ALCOHOLISM: the Nutritional Approach

Alcoholism

The Nutritional Approach

By Roger J. Williams

University of Texas Press   Austin & London

International Standard Book Number 0-292-70301-5
Library of Congress Catalog Card Number 58-59850

Fifth Paperback Printing, 1978

To Alcoholics Anonymous

Preface

PROGRESS IN THE SOLUTION OF the highly important problem of alcoholism has been hampered by considerable confusion with respect to ways and means of advance.

The attitude of the medical profession is of great interest and is certainly an index to the true state of affairs. Most physicians prefer not to have alcoholics among their patients, for the simple reason that doctors are aware of their inability to help alcoholics with their basic problem. Most medical men and laymen consider alcoholism a psychological problem. Many therefore look to psychiatry for help, but here, too, in vain, because few psychiatrists welcome alcoholic patients. The most consistent advice given alcoholics by the medical profession is "Join Alcoholics Anonymous." This, in the writer's opinion, is excellent advice, because Alcoholics Anonymous has a most enviable record for effective work.

This advice when looked at objectively is, however, phenomenal. Is there a parallel in the case of any other disease, for treatment of which physicians refer sick people to a lay group? Obviously this is a state of affairs that would not exist if there were a recognized medical treatment for the disease.

We believe that through biochemical studies we have discovered important causes of this disease, and that advance toward prevention, if not cure, can be expected to be rapid. We do not wish, however, to overemphasize biochemistry and physiology to the exclusion of psychology. We are convinced that people are not built in separate compartments—anatomical, biochemical, psychological—but that they are integrated in such a way that alcoholism, for example, has its roots in every aspect of an individual's make-up.

In the past seven years since an earlier volume dealing with nutrition and alcoholism was published, there have been new discoveries, with a substantial increase in insight into the disease. These I have tried to set forth in the present volume. While there are many worth-while ideas in the earlier volume, it carried an implication—namely that alcoholics might well look forward to a life of moderate drinking—which I cannot now endorse. If an alcoholic is able to drink moderately for a time, this is strong evidence that his appetite has been changed. However, at the present time in the actual handling of alcoholics, the risks of reversion are too great. The dedication of this volume to Alcoholics Anonymous is testimony of the fact that my advice to alcoholics now coincides with that of this organization, namely that alcoholics should abstain. I believe that by nutritional means we can help tremendously in achieving this end.

The greatest hope for the future lies, I believe, in the prevention of the disease. This is a goal which I believe physicians, social workers, the National Council on Alcoholism, members of Alcoholics Anonymous, church groups, and all other interested parties can endorse. Since the preventive means which we emphasize are nutritional, it is fitting and proper that they be sought out and presented by one whose life work has been predominantly in the field of nutritional biochemistry. While the nutritional means which we outline in this book will be found, we believe, to be basic and highly effective for eliminating physiological craving, this does not mean that we minimize the use of educational, religious, psychological, social, or other means to help alcoholics meet the other problems which are not possessed by alcoholics alone, but are common to humanity.

We hope that this volume may effectively promote the cooperation of physicians, ministers, and others who may deal with alcoholics and of research workers who will help ferret out more fully and adequately the basic factors which contribute to this devastating disease. We think that the future looks bright, and that so far as the scientific side is concerned, the disease can be controlled and, even better, prevented, provided we work at the problems with our eyes wide open to the facts which are here presented.

Acknowledgments

It is a pleasure to acknowledge my extreme indebtedness to the Clayton Foundation for Research, which has made possible financially, our whole exploration into the disease alcoholism.

I want also to express my heartfelt thanks to my colleagues, co-workers, and consultants who have contributed to the improvement of this volume: Marty Mann, Richard J. Pelton, Lorene L. Rogers, William Shive, Frank S. Siegel, Frederick J. Stare, Alice M. Timmerman, Arnold E. Williams, M. Phyllis Williams, and Robert R. Williams.

Contents

ALCOHOLISM: the Nutritional Approach

I. What Is Alcoholism?

A SIMPLE DEFINITION of alcoholism is "a tendency to drink too much alcohol." Since some are convinced that any amount of alcohol consumed is "too much," the definition needs clarification—*too much* for what?

It seems obvious that there are all degrees of alcoholism and that drawing a hard and fast line between what is alcoholism and what is not is difficult or impossible. I would say, however, that anyone who drinks enough alcohol to interfere with his or her activities as a useful and productive citizen is a victim of alcoholism. If this interference is slight—and can be guaranteed to remain so—the case is mild. If the interference with productive work is serious, then the case of alcoholism is correspondingly severe.

One of the most difficult barriers to the successful treatment of alcoholism is the fact that many drinkers who are commonly regarded as alcoholics by everyone who knows them will not admit to themselves, or at least to their friends, that the difficulty exists. Undoubtedly this attitude is in part a reaction to the moral stigma that for many decades has been placed on alcoholism.

Looking at the problem in the common-sense manner which I have indicated—namely that alcoholism is simply a tendency to drink too much alcohol—should make it possible for individuals who have any difficulty whatever in this connection to face their own cases in a true light, and not to be too proud to take ameliorative measures. It is my opinion that there are vast numbers of people who have some alcoholic tendencies—even though they may be slight—and that in many cases these tendencies are of such a nature that they can be corrected.

When one thinks of alcoholism, *severe* cases come to mind, and any discussion of the subject must include a consideration of such individuals who have, in general, followed one of two courses—either abstinence (most often with the help of Alcoholics Anonymous) or else the other alternative, ruination followed ultimately by death from diseases associated with excessive alcohol consumption.

It should be made clear at this point that alcoholism is an affliction of *individuals*. No social group is ever afflicted with alcoholism. Families, clans, and communities never become alcoholic; it is specific individuals within these groups who are victims. This is not to deny that a tendency toward alcoholism may be familial or to say that members of certain ethnic groups, such as American Indians, may not be peculiarly susceptible to the affliction. Among the Western European peoples and the cultures in which alcoholic consumption is widespread, alcoholism undoubtedly strikes certain individuals with devastating effects just as certainly as it misses other individuals completely.

Furthermore it is a fact attested by everyone familiar with the problem that those individuals who are strongly alcoholism-prone are in a sense marked men (or women) for life. They never are wholly out of danger so far as the affliction is concerned and "must watch their step" continually as long as they live. This susceptibility is clearly an individual matter. Lack of susceptibility is also an individual matter and there are those who can drink moderately (or even immoderately) for decades without ever practicing the compulsive drinking that is characteristic of severe alcoholism. There are others for whom alcoholic beverages have very little or no attraction even though they are exposed to the use of these beverages.

One of the few uniformities observed in connection with alcoholism is the triggering action of a single drink. Alcoholics may have a craving for alcohol during periods of abstinence (some do more than others), but when after such a period they imbibe even a little, the triggering effect of this first drink is unmistakable. Every victim of alcoholism I have ever heard of has experienced this reaction to alcohol, and this appears to be the one thing common to all those who are afflicted with the condition. An individual who is not alcoholism-prone can take one drink, or more than one, and stop at any predetermined point. An alcoholism-prone individual, especially a severe case, is unable to stop of his own volition once he has started—each drink calls for one more.

Related to the fact that alcoholism is a condition in which specific individuals are involved is the observation that each victim of alcoholism exhibits his own distinctive individual characteristics. Not only are there widely varying degrees of susceptibility, but in the severe cases the results of alcoholism are highly diverse. The periodic drinkers constitute a striking example. Some of these may abstain for weeks or months with seemingly no difficulty. Yet when the desire strikes them and they get the triggering effect of the first drink, they are quite helpless and constitute some of the most severe cases.

The fact that individuals differ in their responses to alcoholic intoxication is notorious and has been recognized for centuries. Thomas Nashe in the sixteenth

6

century classified drunkards into eight kinds: ape drunks, lion drunks, swine drunks, sheep drunks, maudlin drunks, martin drunks, goat drunks, and fox drunks. While one might wish to question or revise this ancient classification, it emphasizes the diversity of human responses and the impossibility of making a detailed description of what the "typical alcoholic" is like. Such a creature doesn't exist. Alcoholics have only one thing in common—an urge (of whatever sort or origin) to drink too much.

II. Drinking in Relation to Other Life Activities

F̲OR SEVERAL YEARS I have been induc-
ing individuals to play what I have called a game of
"Utopia," which involves selecting "baggage" for a
trip to an imaginary paradise.[1]

From a long list of supposedly desirable items such
as athletic activities, physical beauty, card games,

[1] Roger J. Williams, *Free and Unequal* (Austin, University of
Texas Press, 1953), p. 54.

conversation, food, loafing, marriage, music of all kinds, puzzles, reading, religious worship, shows, etc., etc., I have induced them individually and separately to rate each of these items at various levels of desirability from 0 to 10.

A number of different groups of individuals have played such a game anonymously and as a result it becomes perfectly clear that each individual has a remarkably distinctive pattern of likes and dislikes. One individual will put card games high on his list; others will rate them zero. One may rate conversation 10; another 0, 1, or 2. Some consider eating as one of the prime joys of life; others would just as soon swallow their food in capsule form if this were feasible. Some rate loafing and solitude as highly desirable; others leave this baggage item at the dock. As to marriage, some rate it the highest possible; others rate it as of mediocre or less importance.

If one lists the items for each individual in order of the indicated preferences, he gets a high distinctive order of listing for each individual. No two preference lists resemble each other in more than a few items; and the differences between two individuals are never trifling. Even when the individuals are people with similar interests—science students for example—the diversity between them is no less astounding than for a decidedly heterogeneous group. Individuals also vary greatly in the number of items that they rate high.

It seems obvious that these satisfaction-giving items constitute an important key to the pleasure and satisfactions which one gets out of life. Within limits, and other things being equal, the person who rates many different items high is one whose life is full and rich. Those individuals whose list of enjoyments is very limited are liable to be bored unless the kind of activities they enjoy are of such a nature as to be readily available, harmless, and capable of being indulged in for long periods of time.

When the use of alcoholic beverages was included in the list of "baggage" items, the results were similar; some rated it high, others intermediate or zero. It seems clear that anyone who rates alcohol consumption high and who has relatively few other comparable items on his list is in more danger of becoming an alcoholic than one who has many "eggs in his basket." One who is beggar-poor with respect to the number of things he can take satisfaction in, other things being equal, is more vulnerable to the disease of alcoholism.

The importance of this point of view was impressed upon me by my experience with one alcoholic whom we tried to help. This individual apparently had no substantial interest in his business, in religion, in reading, in sex, in food, in travel, in art, in shows, in gardening, in citizenship, or in any of the many things that other people find absorbing. The one thing he appeared to live and care for was liquor and barroom associations. To expect him to give up liquor was like asking a professional southpaw baseball pitcher to part with his left arm. As nearly as I could analyze his case, he didn't have a real desire to give up drink because it was his whole life. There would be nothing left if this were taken away. His behavior seemed at least to bespeak his attitude; he would not cooperate for his own betterment and, in spite of his superb physique, he died at an early age from his excesses. I think it is probable that even with present knowledge he was capable, physiologically, of being helped, but his life pattern was such that he didn't want help. I am sure that he is by no means an isolated case, and that there are hosts of other alcoholics who are unwilling (as he appeared to be) to give up excessive alcohol consumption.

From this point of view it appears that one way to combat alcoholism is to enrich people's lives, so they will have an effective substitute for alcohol if and when they are free (even temporarily) from the clutches of the disease. This is one of the strong points of the Alcoholics Anonymous program.

Enriching people's lives is a more complicated process, however, than may be imagined, because one without an ear (or soul) for music cannot cultivate a passion for it, one without artistic sense cannot become a devotee of art, one without inventiveness cannot thrill to his own inventions, and one with impaired eyesight is not likely to become a great reader. It seems a hard thing to say, but I believe it is true, that some people do not have it in them to be "religious" in the sense that others do, and hence the religious appeal falls on a good many deaf ears. This seems to have been the case throughout recorded history and helps

11

explain why the Alcoholics Anonymous approach (which often has a religious flavor) does not work uniformly.

In order to enrich people's lives we need to know what their potentialities are and what kinds of enrichment they can take. You can enrich the life of a duck by giving it a pond in which to swim, but to enrich the life of a hen, keep her out of the wet and give her dirt to scratch in. On the basis of my explorations into the "want lists" of people I have become convinced that they are in some ways as diverse in their make-ups as are hens and ducks. There is no simple formula for life enrichment which will work for all.

III. Why Do We Drink Alcohol?

THE URGES WHICH CAUSE human beings to drink alcohol may be of several entirely different sorts, and all of these enter into the diverse ratings that individuals give alcohol as a "baggage item" for life's journey.

Some people drink alcohol because they very much like the taste of it. Among the seventy-two small children tested by Richter,[1] six liked samples containing

[1] C. P. Richter, "Alcohol as a Food," *Quarterly Journal of Studies on Alcohol,* Vol. 1, No. 4 (1941), pp. 650–660.

up to 50 per cent alcohol the first time they tasted them. Some alcoholics have told me that this was their experience. Some other individuals may not like it at first but cultivate a liking for it.

Other individuals may not particularly like the taste of alcohol, but they like the effect that it produces. It seems to release their tensions, make them forget their troubles, make it possible for them to have a good time, to be uninhibited, to say and do things that they otherwise would not say or do. It makes their drinking companions tolerant and appreciative, too; the conversation seems more interesting all around and the jokes funnier. Some drinkers—even cases of severe alcoholism—insist that they do not like the taste of alcohol. In fact they dislike it. Yet they drink it consistently because, as most psychologists interpret it, it allows them to escape from many things in their lives that haunt them.

Another factor causing some people to drink alcohol is social pressure—it seems the thing to do. "Men of distinction" set them a pattern, and they tend to follow it whether they get any particular pleasure out of the drinks or not. If it were not for the satisfaction they get from being a member of a drinking group, the disadvantages of drinking might easily appear to outweigh the advantages.

The social pressure which often develops with respect to drinking is a phenomenon which has its roots in the fact that some individuals greatly enjoy drinking. If this liking did not exist, the social pressure would never develop. People never are under social pressure to sit around sucking the ends of corn cobs, smoking alfalfa leaves, or drinking the tea made from eucalyptus leaves. There is nothing in any of these operations that has an appeal for anyone. No one (so far as I know) likes to do these things. It is therefore evident that when we say that people drink merely because of social pressure, we are oversimplifying the situation. The social pressure stems from the fact that some people like alcohol and/or its effects.

In addition to and superimposed upon these reasons for drinking is another one which must be recognized and understood if we are to have a thorough grasp of the problem of alcoholism. Why do some individuals have an urge to drink on and on, while others can stop at any time they want to? Is it because the on-and-on drinkers like alcohol so much better than the majority of people? This cannot be the answer because some severe alcoholics definitely do not like the taste of alcohol. Is it because some individuals have more troubles than others and the ones who need so badly to escape are the ones who become alcoholics? Some will probably answer yes to this question but in my experience it is a wholly inadequate answer. I have encountered too many severe alcoholics who had happy homes, who were happy in their work, and appeared to be less in need of escape than most, and yet they were alcoholics. On the other hand, I'm sure there are others who have had tremendous need for escape, but are not at all inclined toward alcoholism. Without question alcohol

15

does things to some people that it doesn't do to others. Some people drink it for reasons that do not apply to others.

In order to understand the alcoholism problem fully we need to be able to answer, among others, this question: *Why does one drink call for another?* Is it that the succeeding drinks taste so much better than the initial one? Is it that an individual having made a partial escape from his troubles has a greatly augmented desire to escape further? Is it that social pressure mounts up, so that one gains in prestige with each succeeding drink?

Though there may be some grains of truth in these suggestions, they are in my opinion wholly inadequate to explain the tremendous urge which alcoholics have and which other individuals largely escape. Alcohol is a physiological agent and the urge which the initial drink produces, in my opinion, arises because of *deranged cellular metabolism*. Except for the fact that derangement is involved, the urge is fundamentally similar to the urge we have for water when our tissues become dehydrated, for salt when our tissues become salt-hungry, for food when our tissues are starving, for calcium when we are deficient in this element because of parathyroid malfunctioning. It is fundamentally like our urge to eat candy when we are candy-hungry (though much stronger) or the unfortunate craving some diabetics have for sugar or the ravenous hunger for yeast which a vitamin B–deficient animal exhibits.

The experience of "internal tremor" that heavy

consumers of alcohol may have after a spree is a case in point. Whatever the reason ascribed for going on the spree, whether social pressure, "psychotrauma," or something else, it is rarely denied that hang-over or "internal tremor" is physical torment. A common remedy for this physical discomfort is more alcohol—"hair from the dog that bit you." This vicious use of alcohol for hang-over represents a step toward severe alcoholism, and is brought about by a bodily condition. The appetite-controlling mechanisms are seriously deranged; not only is there a desire for alcohol but there often is an extreme aversion to food, something that every cell in the body really needs.

If the phenomenon of "more calling for more" were unique for alcohol, we might be justified in trying to explain it on some specific psychological basis, rather than on a physiological one. However, morphine, cocaine, and nicotine, for example, are habit-forming drugs with effects which are very much the same as alcohol in one respect—one shot produces an appetite for more of the same. Undoubtedly these agents have a physiological poisoning effect on certain regulatory cells and tissues of the body, and, as a result, the individual craves morphine, cocaine, or nicotine in the same sense that he would crave water if he were on the desert without a drink. It is neither a psychological nor an intelligent craving. It is a deranged *physiological craving induced by a physiological agent.*

There is then, in my opinion, another reason why people may drink alcohol aside from their liking for it or for its effects and aside from social pressure. This fourth reason is a deranged physiological urge or craving. Their "body wisdom" is impaired; it has turned into "body foolishness"; the body demands are no longer a safe guide; the more its demands are indulged the worse its condition becomes. This deranged physiological urge is made more acute if an individual who is subject to it takes even a small drink. This small drink, probably by acting as a specific poison to a weakened hypothalamus (a portion of the brain which is related to appetites), pulls a physiological trigger in an alcoholic which may lead to devastating results. The physiological urge to drink, this foolishness of the body, is most easily produced in the most severe alcoholics, and most difficult to produce in those for whom alcohol is no problem. This fact is the basis for the saying that it is all right to take a drink when you *want* one, but not when you *need* one. Those who have never had this specific craving for alcohol are unable to understand the problem that an alcoholic has, just as those who have never been morphine addicts cannot understand the craving that dope addicts possess.

Of course alcohol is a unique substance, in that, unlike most drugs, it can serve as a fuel for the body. It is double-barreled in its activity; it serves as a source of energy—like sugar—but at the same time it (or substances to which it is transformed in the body) acts as a poison to derange the appetite mechanisms of the body, thereby destroying appetite for food and inducing a perverted physiological craving for alcohol.

Why Do We Drink Alcohol?

The utilization of alcohol as a fuel is a very interesting process; alcohol is a ready source of energy and its utilization does not involve as much biochemical processing as does the utilization of many other substances. For this reason, not so many enzymes are involved and the needs for the raw materials out of which the enzymes are built may not be so exacting when alcohol is used for fuel. This appears to be the case for some individuals who over a period of years are able to substitute alcohol for food to a surprising degree, and yet remain comparatively well. This is something that it is impossible to understand unless we take into account the *tremendous biochemical individuality* that exists.

This ready utilization of alcohol which for some individuals takes place with relatively few damaging side effects, may be a factor in the development of a desire to drink. Our bodies, like us as individuals, are "on the lookout" for easy ways to do things and for some of our bodies, alcohol offers a relatively easy source of energy. Biochemical individuality is the factor which prevents, as we shall see more clearly later, many individuals from taking this easy route.

In summary we may say that individuals may drink alcohol because of a liking for it, because of a liking for its relaxing and other effects, because of social pressure, or because of a physiological urge to drink. This physiological urge or craving is particularly important in the problem of alcoholism, for without it typical alcoholism probably would not exist.

IV. What Our Bodies Need

ᗷECAUSE it is increasingly apparent that the problem of alcoholism is related to nutrition, it is important for all those who study the subject to be aware of the why's and the wherefore's of nutrition and its place in the general scheme of things.

The life of each of us begins as a single fertilized egg cell. This cell divides and subdivides on and on until billions of marvelously coordinated cells of many kinds are produced. The original fertilized egg cell has tremendous potentialities. In it reside thousands of heritable qualities of the individual-to-be—its sex, body size, and many distinctive anatomical features, external and internal, which each of us possesses at the time of birth.

If this developing organism—including all of its parts—is continuously furnished everything that it needs, it develops to maturity, and, unless various kinds of accidents intervene, it lives a long span of years.

The various items that this organism must be supplied from without can be listed under four headings: (1) oxygen (air), (2) water, (3) a suitable degree of warmth, and (4) chemical raw materials (food) out of which the organism can build itself. No developing organism can create matter or produce something from nothing. These bodily needs have some resemblance to the elements of the ancient Greeks: air, water, fire, and earth.

Many other substances not included in the above list enter in a vital way into the life of every higher organism, notably enzymes and hormones, but these are produced within the organism from the nutritional elements which are furnished by the food.

Of the four kinds of needs listed, the first three are relatively simple, but the last—food—is complicated, not only because organisms often need a complex assortment of food substances, but also because different *kinds* of organisms always have highly distinctive needs. Furthermore the nutritional needs of a given organism at one stage of development may be different from the needs at an earlier or later stage.

Human nutritional needs may be listed under four headings (1) fuel, (2) minerals, (3) amino acids derived from proteins, and (4) vitamins. All of these needs are absolute. No animal or human has ever, in the long history of living things, developed from a fertilized egg unless during the course of development it received from sources outside itself *all* of these essentials.

We need not discuss in detail the kinds of fuel that our human bodies burn. The fuel requirement is not very exacting. Carbohydrates, proteins, fats, or even alcohol can be burned. Gasoline doesn't work.

The minerals which are essential to our life include calcium, phosphorus, potassium, sodium, chlorine, iodine, magnesium, iron, copper, manganese, zinc, cobalt, molybdenum, fluorine, and perhaps a few others. Some of these are required in minute amounts, probably for catalytic purposes, as will be discussed later in this chapter; others are needed in larger amounts for structural uses. It is important that no human organism ever lived or thrived without the availability of *every one* of these essentials in adequate amounts.

The amino acids which we must get in our food, usually from proteins, include: valine, leucine, isoleucine, threonine, methionine, lysine, phenylalanine, and tryptophane. Other amino acids are also desirable as food constituents, and still others doubtless fill an absolute need under some circumstances. To persons who are not trained in biochemistry or medicine the designations above are merely names; but the substances are real, and our needs for adequate amounts of each are real. No human being has ever developed, nor can one maintain life, unless each of these foods is furnished in sufficient amounts.

The vitamins are characteristically needed in very small amounts, and their function is to help speed up certain chemical reactions which would otherwise take place far too slowly to allow life to exist. Most chemical reactions taking place in our bodies need catalysts or "hasteners" to speed them up. Since a multitude of reactions take place in our bodies, many, many catalysts are needed. The numerous vitamins and "trace elements" are necessary components of the hasteners which make life possible.

The need for vitamins is universal and absolute. No organism ever gets along without them. Some lower forms can make the vitamins they need from simpler substances, but human beings, and other mammals, absolutely require a wide assortment. Some poorly informed people may think of vitamins as a recent fad. It is true that we have known about them for only a few decades, but there is abundant evidence that they have been part of nature's equipment since long before man appeared on earth.

It is highly important that we recognize the need, not only for *some* of every nutritional item, but for *enough* of every one. In some cases "enough" is a very small amount, but half enough is too little and the lack of the full amount may be almost as serious as a total lack. We may need as little as a thousandth of an ounce of iodine, spread over an entire lifetime. In this case if we received only one two-thousandth, we would suffer from iodine deficiency. The same principle holds for every other item in the long list of nutritional needs.

Do we need just enough and is there danger of getting too much of some of the items? Regarding fuel, it is true that our capacity for burning it is limited and if we take in too much, dire results may ensue. Our natural appetites take care of this problem to a large degree and we are prevented by this means from taking on several times what we can use.

With respect to many other nutritional elements— minerals, amino acids, and vitamins—there is often a wide margin of safety between what we need and what will harm us. Even salt or water can produce bad effects if taken in excessive quantities, but there is a wide margin of safety and our appetites usually intervene to protect us. A few *milligrams* of copper is needed every day. A few *grams* of a copper salt— roughly a thousand times what we need—will cause vomiting and may even cause death. A similar amount of zinc is needed each day; a thousand times this amount will cause vomiting. In these cases the margin is wide enough so there is little cause for concern.

If we were to give the vitamin thiamine (B_1) to a dog in amounts 100,000 times as great as the dog's daily needs, it might cause death. This is a very wide margin. Some other vitamins, for example, riboflavin (B$_2$) and pantothenate (B$_3$), have never been found to be toxic to animals in any amounts used. In one experiment, monkeys, which need perhaps two milligrams of B$_3$ daily, were given five hundred times this amount every day for six months without any noticeable bad effects. In these cases the excess vitamin which is not built into enzymes is merely eliminated or burned and does no harm.

The maxim "if a little is good, more is better" cannot be applied over a wide range with respect to trace minerals and vitamins, since it is definitely possible to take too much of the trace elements or even of vitamins. However, in dealing with these items if one follows reasonable directions and avoids "eating" supplies which were intended to be used only as nutritional supplements, the danger is negligible. The expense involved is sufficient to discourage one from serious overdosage in most cases. Dosages set by competent authorities should always be followed.

When one is concerned with amino acids or minerals which are needed in much larger amounts, the danger from the ill effects of overdosage would be greater were it not for the expensiveness of the items and the natural reluctance of people to take into their bodies large quantities of any unfamiliar (or distasteful) chemical. We will discuss this problem further in a later chapter.

It needs to be emphasized at this point that our bodies need, not single food elements by themselves, but a suitable assortment of all. When we say *all*, we mean *all*. If one single food element is missing from our diet, our bodies fail to get what they need. They suffer from malnutrition just as truly as if many items were missing.

What happens when our bodies fail to get enough of everything they need? The results depend on which particular food element is in short supply, and how severe the shortage is. A healthy animal (or human being) can be completely deprived of an essential food for several days without any outwardly observable harm, because the healthy organism has its own supply to start with and the deprivation does not become serious at once. If an animal (or human being) is supplied continuously, for example, with 20 per cent less of a particular food substance than it needs for optimal performance, it will not die; in fact, in most cases there will be no clinical manifestation of deficiency. Nevertheless the life of the organism will be somewhat impaired by this lack and some of the organs and tissues will suffer more than others.

It is sometimes not appreciated that every cell and tissue of the body (there are billions of cells and hundreds of different kinds of cells) require constant nutrition. Each kind of cell has its distinctive requirements. Nutrition is not for "the body as a whole" but for every cell. Each cell has its own functions. While we have enough cells of each kind so that not all of them have to work at top efficiency, the effects of mild malnutrition cannot safely be disregarded by those who would enjoy maximum health. The mills of the gods grind slowly but they grind exceedingly fine, and it is probable that in this modern day more ills are caused by mild or severe cellular malnutrition than by any other cause. One can appear perfectly normal in looks and in behavior and yet be the victim of mild cellular malnutrition, which may impair the activity of important functioning tissues and decrease one's bodily efficiency materially.

Finally we must emphasize that nutritional knowledge has not advanced to the point where we even know every nutritional factor by name; much less do we know about how much of each particular item is needed, or the ready sources for each. To satisfy an individual's nutritional needs is not always easy. If the needs are unusual, a certain amount of good fortune has to be involved in order to attain complete success.

V. Control Mechanisms in Relation to Diet

IN OUR BODIES are a number of control mechanisms which help us to keep on a relatively even keel. For example, there is a temperature-controlling center in the brain which acts like a thermostat and helps us maintain a body temperature which is relatively constant. In fever this mechanism is out of order. There is likewise a "respiratory center" in the brain which controls breathing. When the blood becomes a little less alkaline than it should be, this stimulates the respiratory center, which in turn activates the breathing muscles, and carbon dioxide is pumped out by way of the lungs until the blood is back to normal.

When we exercise and perspire freely our tissues become dehydrated, but we do not have to consult a physician to know the remedy. Our mouths, tongues, and throats ultimately get the message; we are induced to drink water until the dehydration is counteracted—then we aren't thirsty any more.

From the standpoint of our discussion, however, one of the most interesting control mechanisms is that involved in telling us how much to eat. How much we eat and absorb is governed automatically in many individuals with almost unbelievable accuracy. For example there are individuals who during the course of twenty years of adult life may gain or lose less than ten pounds and at the same time they may give the matter of weight control no thought whatever. During this twenty years they may consume as much as forty thousand pounds of moist food. This means that the weight balance between income and outgo over the years is subject to an error of less than one-fortieth of 1 per cent! This has happened millions of times historically and prehistorically, even long before pounds or calories were invented. For the people involved it is an automatic process which may require no conscious attention.

The exact details of how this mechanism works

(Jolliffe calls it the "appestat")[1] are not fully known, but it seems clear that the hypothalamus of the brain is involved, because, for example, artificially produced lesions in the hypothalamus may cause experimental animals to exaggerate their eating tremendously and become highly obese. The cells and tissues of the body themselves are part of the mechanism which controls eating. When they lack food they cry out for it, and no matter how the message gets to its destination, the effect is the same—hunger and the desire to eat.

It is clear that the individuality, which we have discussed earlier, is applicable in this realm, because not all people have as perfect mechanisms as the individuals we have cited. Some adult individuals will, if they eat all they want, gain weight continuously until they are highly obese, thereby demonstrating that something is wrong with the automatic mechanism at some point—maybe in some of the tissues, maybe in the hypothalamus, maybe somewhere else.

It is a well-recognized fact that there are in our bodies specific mechanisms which not only control the total number of calories consumed but also help control the amounts of specific food elements which we consume. Salt is an example of such a food element. To a degree, our body mechanisms tell us not only how much to eat but what to eat. Although "salt hunger" is not common among populations with which we are more familiar, there are regions in Africa, I have been

[1] N. Jolliffe, *Reduce and Stay Reduced* (New York, Simon and Schuster, 1952).

30

told by personal observers, where salt is scarce, and a gift of a piece of rock salt would be prized more highly by children than a gift of candy. The diet of herbivorous animals is such as to induce salt shortage in their tissues and their blood, and as a result they develop salt hunger and may travel for many miles in search of a "salt lick" or an artificial source. The adrenal glands are a part of the mechanism which controls salt consumption. Rats which have damaged adrenal glands exhibit salt hunger and are able to detect salt in dilute solution at much lower levels than when their adrenal glands are intact.

Hunger for calcium and phosphorus can be altered in experimental animals by modifying the activity of the parathyroid glands. These glands help control the calcium level of the blood and affect in a reciprocal manner the phosphate usage. When the parathyroid glands are injured or removed, the calcium level of the blood drops, calcium hunger is induced and an aversion to phosphate develops. Phosphate consumption would deplete the calcium further and the mouth is, in effect, notified to reject phosphate.

Depletion of animals with respect to the B vitamins contained in yeast will cause them to have a hunger seemingly somewhat specific. If such a depleted animal is given a tiny taste of yeast, it will exhibit extreme excitement and will be ravenous for more.

It must not be assumed, however, that animals or human beings have perfect regulatory mechanisms that always tell them exactly what to eat. This is far from the case; otherwise there would be no need to study nutrition, and the condition with which we are concerned—alcoholism—would not exist. It is obvious that in some individuals automatic choices are often very unfortunate ones. For all of us some automatic choices are likely to be wrong.

What can be wrong with a bodily mechanism which controls the consumption of water, calories, salt, calcium, or any other food element for which there is control? It can be malformed anatomically; it can be infected or poisoned by some outside agent; it can be deficient biochemically with respect to something it needs for its proper operation. Combinations of these difficulties may exist together.

What can we do for an ailing mechanism of this sort? If malformation is involved, we may be able to supply completely the missing agent, as we do when we administer thyroid hormone or insulin. If infection or poisoning is involved, we may be able to get rid of the infection or eliminate the poison; if there is a biochemical deficiency, we may be able to supply the biochemical need which in turn may make possible normal functioning and increased resistance to infection and to poisoning.

An important point which I wish to emphasize is that these control mechanisms all have an anatomical and physiological basis and that cellular malnutrition may be an important factor in inducing malfunctioning of any control mechanism regardless of just where it is located or how intricate its workings may be.

To cite some definite evidence on this point let us consider another specific food substance, sugar. If—to take a purely hypothetical case—one were to be intellectually convinced that he needed above all things and at once, a pound of sugar, he would find it impossible to "convince his body" of this fact sufficiently to make its consumption possible. The first ounce of sugar might be palatable, but in a short time one's body would begin to revolt and sugar would become nauseating. This wisdom of the body is a very real control mechanism.

Malnutrition, however, can impair this wisdom of the body and transform the wisdom into foolishness. Macy in her extended study of child nutrition[2] found that children who were consuming relatively poor diets consumed more sugar (when given a voluntary choice) than did children on better diets. Malnutrition had the effect of damaging the control mechanism (in the hypothalamus or elsewhere) so that the wisdom of the body was decreased.

We have demonstrated positively the same thing in experimental animals (rats) kept in individual cages and given a choice between two drinks—water and sugar water.[3] The effects of different diets on this

[2] Icie G. Macy, *Nutrition and Chemical Growth in Childhood* (Springfield, Illinois, and Baltimore, Maryland, Charles C. Thomas, I, 1942), p. 84.

[3] Roger J. Williams, R. B. Pelton, and L. L. Rogers, "Dietary Deficiencies in Animals in Relation to Voluntary Alcohol and Sugar Consumption," *Quarterly Journal of Studies on Alcohol,* Vol. 16, No. 2 (1955), pp. 234–244.

choice were studied extensively, and there is no question that the poorer diet caused increased sugar consumption; this in turn caused the total calorie consumption to be of an even poorer quality—progressively more deficient in amino acids, minerals, and vitamins. The only reasonable interpretation is that cellular malnutrition decreased the wisdom of the body of the rats and affected adversely the hypothalamus or some other part of the mechanism which they possess for governing sugar consumption. The fact that good nutrition promotes good nutrition seems a variation of the biblical saying, "To him that hath shall be given." Well-nourished animals or human beings have more body wisdom than poorly nourished ones, and they tend to stay well-nourished for this reason. Poorly nourished animals or human beings when given a free choice can easily get into a vicious cycle whereby poor nutrition leads to further poor nutrition.

VI. Biochemical Individuality
—An Inescapable Factor

WHEN AN EARLIER BOOK on the subject of alcoholism was written, information about biochemical individuality was scanty and not wholly clear. Since that time much convincing evidence has been accumulated, and has been brought together in a separate volume.[1] Numerous references and further

[1] Roger J. Williams, *Biochemical Individuality* (New York, John Wiley and Sons, 1956).

details regarding the phenomena mentioned here may be found in that book.

The large body of evidence for this individuality rests upon not only (1) gross and microscopic anatomical variations but also on (2) differences in blood and body composition, (3) differences in enzyme levels, (4) differences in endocrine activities, (5) differences in excretion patterns, (6) differences in responses to drugs and chemicals, and (7) differences in nutritional needs. In each one of these areas there may be found items for which the differences between "normal" individuals are not 25 to 50 per cent but actually 500 to 1000 per cent! Even wider variations than these are not infrequent.

The bloods of two normal individuals collected under the same basal conditions may vary with respect to their content of specific fat-like substances by as much as eight- to sixteenfold. The acetylcholine and histamine contents of normal blood samples vary at least eightfold. The gastric juice of one normal individual may have 400 times as much pepsin in it as that of his normal neighbor. We are different even in our bones—the density of the bones of some normal young men has been found in very careful X-ray studies to be 5.7 times as great as that of other normal young men of the same age group.

Most of the chemical reactions taking place in our bodies are mediated by specific enzymes (catalysts) which our bodies produce. The amounts of these enzymes in the blood give us some idea of the rates at which the different chemical reactions take place. Five enzymes have been studied from this standpoint with sufficient thoroughness so that we can say that the levels vary markedly and are characteristic for each individual. Alkaline phosphatase levels vary in normal individuals over at least a fivefold range; choline esterase levels vary similarly over about a threefold range; for the arginase in corpuscles the range is at least about fourfold; for serum amylase, fiftyfold (!) ; for β-glucuronidase, at least tenfold.

These objectively determined facts, even when considered alone, show clearly that the body chemistry of each of us is distinctive and that the differences in the patterns of metabolism are of great magnitude and by no means minor or trifling.

Endocrine glands vary widely from individual to individual. Thyroid glands, for example, may vary in weight, among normal individuals, from 8 to 50 grams; the parathyroids (two to twelve in number) vary in weight from 50 to 300 milligrams. The testes in normal males weigh from 10 to 45 grams; the ovaries in females vary in weight from 2 to 10 grams and contain at birth from 30,000 to 400,000 ova. The pineal glands weigh from 50 to 400 milligrams, and pancreas glands contain from 200,000 to 2,500,000 islets of Langerhans where insulin is produced. The adrenal cortices of different individuals are said to vary about tenfold in thickness. It should be emphasized that the values given above are "normal" ones. Other values outside the above ranges are not infrequently encountered, but they are regarded as abnormal.

Bloodhounds can distinguish one individual person from another by odors, and it is not surprising that the urinary composition is distinctive for each individual. The percentages of the following substances, for example, in urinary contents all vary from normal individual to normal individual by at least tenfold to twenty-fivefold: hippuric acid, taurine, glycine, serine, citrulline. This is further evidence of a high degree of biochemical individuality.

Whenever a chemical or a drug has a physiological or pharmacological effect on an individual, it does so because of an *interaction* between the chemical or drug and some body constituents of the individual. If the *same* drug or chemical affects two people differently, it must be because the body chemistries of the two individuals are not the same.

Among the responses to chemicals which show wide diversity are the taste responses. These involve the specific nerve endings present in the taste buds; and if the taste buds of different individuals were alike in their biochemical functioning, the responses to every chemical would be identical for different individuals.

The majority of people experience an extremely bitter sensation when phenyl thiocarbamide is applied to the tongue. To a minority (from about 0 per cent to about 40 per cent, depending on the ethnic group) it is completely tasteless.

Creatine, a prominent organic muscle constituent,

is bitter to some, tasteless to others. Sodium benzoate to some is tasteless; to others it is bitter; to others sour; to others sweet; and to others salty. Some individuals find saccharin to have 2,000 times the sweetening effect of sugar; to others, it is only 32 times as effective as a sweetening agent. For some, quinine is 256 times as bitter as cascara; for others, it is only one-half as bitter. From 15 per cent of people mannose elicited no taste response, to 20 per cent it was sweet only, to 10 per cent it was bitter only, and to the rest it was sweet and bitter in succession.

Richter has found children who could not detect the sweetness of a 20 per cent sugar solution. He also found as we have already indicated, that seventy-two small children, four to ten years of age, varied greatly in their liking for alcohol of different concentrations. Most of them did not "like the taste" of any concentration above 10 or 15 per cent, but six "liked" samples containing up to 50 per cent alcohol.

In our laboratories we have found that the taste thresholds for such common substances as sodium or potassium chloride often vary, from individual to individual, over at least a hundredfold range. Since all of these observations involve interactions between the specific substances and the taste buds of different individuals, they demonstrate the existence of marked biochemical individuality.

Similar evidence is available with respect to the sense of smell. A potassium cyanide solution has for some a strong odor; for others a weak odor; for still others it has no odor whatever. In an experiment involving 244 people, 24 males out of 132 could not smell such a solution at all; only 5 females out of 112 lacked this ability. Further experiments indicate that the inability to smell potassium cyanide solution is a sex-linked recessive.

Not only are different responses obtained in experiments involving the special senses, but they may be observed in other cases as well. The minimal concentrations of mercuric chloride (a strong poison) required to cause skin irritation in a series of 35 individuals were determined. Only 1 responded to a concentration of 1 part per 100,000, 1 to 3 parts per 100,000, 5 to 10 parts, 11 to 30 parts, 13 to 100 parts, and 4 failed to respond even at this level. This more than hundredfold variation in the effectiveness of a virulent poison on a specific tissue is suggestive with respect to the probable variations in the effects of alcohol on the appetite centers of different individuals.

A recent study was made on 29 healthy young men involving the effects of morphine injection. Saline controls were used. The drug caused nausea in 18, sleep in 16, drunkenness in 9, dizziness in 13, itching in 9, and indistinct speech in 7. It is well known that this drug excites an occasional individual instead of causing depression and that some individuals, unlike others, are prone to become addicts.

Finally, let us consider the intoxicating effects of alcohol itself. Nagle found that 0.25 ounce of alcohol had the same effect on certain individuals as did 10 times the amount on others. Jetter found in a study of 1,000 individuals using objective tests that 10.5 per cent were intoxicated when the alcohol blood level was 0.05 per cent, whereas 6.7 per cent were *sober* when the alcohol blood level was eight times this high—0.4 per cent. Later, a study of 800 more individuals was completed, confirming the earlier observations.

Here again in the field of the action of drugs and chemicals, we find enormous differences in response, indicating clearly that our body chemistries not only differ detectably, but differ enormously.

Serious attempts to study the differences in the nutritional needs of individual people have, in general, never been made. In the course of the study of nutrition, however, a number of such differences have become apparent. In one of the very few studies in which variation in the nutritional needs of normal individuals has been investigated, it was found that among 19 healthy normal young men the requirement for calcium (in order to prevent calcium loss from the body) varied from 3.52 to 16.16 milligrams per kilogram of body weight. This nearly fivefold range in all probability would have been substantially larger if larger numbers of men had been included. Certainly the inclusion of women would be expected to increase the range.

There is evidence, which is too involved to discuss here, that the vitamin A requirement of individual human beings varies at least over a tenfold range. The minimum amount of vitamin D needed by any normal human being is not known, but the maximum is certainly twenty times what is considered average. The best available evidence (which admittedly is not wholly satisfactory) indicates that the variation in thiamin (vitamin B_1) needs is at least fourfold. There seems no question but that the vitamin B_6 requirements of infants vary over a severalfold range. The requirements for vitamin B_{12} vary greatly also and the same is true of niacin and a number of other nutritional factors. The range in the human needs for the amino acid threonine is from one hundred to five hundred milligrams per day as determined on a small group.

All of these facts are perfectly in line with the idea that our body chemistries differ from one another very substantially. We carry out specific chemical reactions at different rates, we have different efficiencies with respect to the reactions we carry out, and we need varying amounts of the various food substances as raw materials for the chemical processes we operate.

In view of what we have had to say about alcoholism as a condition that affects individuals (some are strongly vulnerable, others definitely are not), it seems true beyond a shadow of a doubt that *biochemical individuality (the distinctiveness of our body chemistries) is a factor in the problem.*

While biochemical individuality is undoubtedly an important factor in alcoholism it is by no means a simple matter to elucidate its role. How far we have gone in this direction will be discussed in later chapters.

One encouraging feature of this advance is described in Chapter XII. One of the important objectives of the publication of this book is to enlist as many qualified investigators as possible in the search for the biochemical differences which make for alcoholism-proneness. We do not believe that such a search, if painstakingly carried out, will go unrewarded.

The importance of biochemical individuality does not, as we will attempt to make clear later, rule out the consideration of psychological and sociological factors which may contribute to the downfall of alcoholism-prone individuals or to similar influences, including religion, which may help rehabilitate alcoholics. We advocate a comprehensive, as opposed to a one-sided, approach to the disease.

The neglect of *biochemical individuality* as a factor in alcoholism explains why more progress has not been made in controlling the disease—why most physicians have no treatment to offer. Attention to other factors is by no means reprehensible, but real success in dealing with the difficulty cannot be attained until *all* the important factors are taken into account. In the literature pertaining to alcoholism there are a number of references to the "X factor" involved. What is the "peculiar element" present in the life of alcoholic addicts and absent from the lives of those who can drink moderately?

From the beginning of my study of the problem of alcoholism, I have been convinced that distinctive body chemistries must be involved in the answer to

43

this question and that an important "X factor" (or factors) must lie in this realm. Many of those who have looked at the alcoholism problem in what has become a traditional manner, completely ignore the biochemical individuality which seems clearly to be of great import. This attitude of unawareness, this head-in-the-sand stance, cannot persist indefinitely in the face of the facts which are now apparent. It cannot always be taken as an axiomatic fact that alcoholism is fundamentally a psychological and a psychiatric problem. The psychological factors enter but physiological and biochemical factors are involved too, and to be ignorant of these is to be ignorant of the disease itself. Anyone who attempts to discuss the subject of alcoholism as a whole without regard for biochemical individuality is, in the light of our recently acquired knowledge, clearly attempting the impossible.

Before closing this chapter I want to make clear that our realization of the tremendous scope and significance of biochemical individuality is based upon facts (not theories) which have been brought into the open for consideration only in the past few years. It is my conviction that these facts which are so important for alcoholism are also important (but not to the exclusion of other factors) for a thousand other problems.[2] If they are taken into account fully in connection with the alcoholism problem, this disease will be

[2] Roger J. Williams, "Biochemical Approach to the Study of Personality," *Psychiatric Research Reports* 2 (1955), pp. 31–33.

the first of a long series of human problems to be attacked on the basis of these facts in combination with other recognized causes. Only when these real and absorbing facts of life are laid alongside many others can we have a satisfactory body of information on which to base an attack on many diverse human problems.

VII. The Genetotrophic Concept

G̲ENETOTROPHIC may seem a formidable word. It carries the combination of two ideas—"geneto" referring to genetics or heredity, "trophic" to feeding or nutrition. A genetotrophic difficulty is one that stems from the possession of some unusually high nutritional requirement(s) of genetic origin, *coupled with* a failure to meet this need.[1] The con-

[1] Roger J. Williams, E. Beerstecher, Jr., and L. J. Berry, "The Concept of Genetotrophic Disease," *The Lancet,* I (1950), 287; Roger J. Williams, "Concept of Genetotrophic Disease," *Nutrition Reviews,* Vol. 8, No. 9 (1950), pp. 257–260.

46

cept was based initially upon our experience with rats. If a rat on an ordinary stock diet drank alcohol at high levels and yet could be made to abstain by supplementing its diet with certain food elements, we concluded that the tendency to drink was genetotrophic in origin. When the rat in question was supplied with plenty of the satisfying food elements it had no tendency to drink; on the other hand its drinking tendency would not have been exhibited at all if it had possessed a different genetic background with less exacting nutritional requirements, like those of some of its fellow rats.

It seems clear now that the physiological urge to drink alcohol which some humans possess or develop is genetotrophic in origin. Some individuals have genetic backgrounds which cause them to have high requirements for certain nutritional elements (for different individuals it may be a different nutritional element or a different assortment). This makes the individual vulnerable, and as soon as he drinks alcohol in substantial amount (for social or other reasons) he dilutes his diet, crowds out minerals, amino acids, and vitamins to some extent, and as a result becomes deficient. Each jigger (oz.) of whiskey yields about sixty-four calories and dilutes the daily diet about $2\frac{1}{2}$ per cent. Eight ounces in a day (for some individuals this is a modest amount) dilutes the diet 20 per cent at least. The deficiency which results in specific cases weakens the regulatory tissues in the hypothalamus and thus enhances the poisoning effect of the alcohol on these vulnerable tissues. This impairs the appetite-controlling centers, with the result that body wisdom changes to body foolishness, and no amount of intellectual wisdom is sufficient to counteract the strong physiological urge to drink.

In each of the fertilized egg cells—which constitutes the starting point for each of us—there are the genes, the carriers of heredity. Some of these transmit to the daughter cells the potentiality for producing specific enzymes which are catalysts or hasteners for specific chemical reactions. Individual genes are often intimately concerned with the production of specific enzymes.

All human beings have in their chromosomes the genes necessary to produce the enzymes which are characteristically needed by humans. But there is excellent evidence of the existence of partial genetic blocks, which impair the work of these genes. For this reason, in some individuals the potentiality for producing an enzyme may be present, but only to a limited degree. Such partial impairments are probably very common and are closely tied to the biochemical individuality discussed in the preceding chapter.

The genes never furnish the raw materials out of which enzymes are built; these must be furnished in the food. For enzyme-building, amino acids, trace minerals, and vitamins are often needed. If all of these are furnished in completely adequate amounts, the existence of an impaired gene (especially if not too severe) may be overcome completely.

A person who is afflicted with a genetotrophic disease is one who has by heredity certain partial genetic blocks (or something that operates in a similar fashion) which cause him to need larger amounts of certain nutrients. He is prone to become deficient in certain respects; however, if all his needs are fully and continuously supplied he may be just as healthy as anyone else.

That unusually high demands for specific food substances exist for individuals in the general population is now amply demonstrated. In a previous chapter we have cited as examples calcium, vitamin A, vitamin D, thiamine, vitamin B_6, vitamin B_{12} and the amino acid threonine, in which cases there is evidence of ranges of the order of four- to twentyfold or more from one "normal" individual to another.[2] The idea that some individuals may possess *much higher* requirements for certain food items than others is not just a theory; it is a demonstrated fact.

Personal experiences corroborate this fact and show that not only may individual requirements be unusually high in specific instances, but the unusually high needs may lead to specific health difficulties. Several years ago a scientist told me of his extraordinarily high thiamine requirement. He found that his severe headaches and other difficulties were alleviated when he took capsules containing an assortment of B vitamins. Not content to be relieved, however, he determined to

[2] Roger J. Williams, *Biochemical Individuality,* (New York, John Wiley and Sons, 1956), pp. 143 ff.

49

find what specific ingredient (or ingredients) was responsible. He had capsules made up with different ingredients supplied singly and took them without foreknowledge as to their contents. He was able thus to identify thiamine as the only vitamin which had this effect on him. To maintain good health he found it necessary to take continuously many times the amount of thiamine that is usually considered adequate. Another acquaintance of mine—a physician—told me of a similar high need for thiamine; in this case the deficiency caused difficulties with eyesight.

Another friend discovered by accident an unusual need for pantothenic acid. As soon as abundant amounts of pantothenate were supplied to this person (for greying hair), constipation, which had been a lifelong affliction, disappeared. It recurred when the pantothenate was withdrawn, but was abolished again when pantothenate was readministered. For this person extra pantothenate was "invaluable."

A scientist friend also observed an unusual need for pantothenic acid in connection with a very different difficulty. He was subject to allergy—hay fever—and was particularly susceptible to the dust and pollen which he encountered in certain desert regions. When he took continuously a high dosage of calcium pantothenate his allergy disappeared and he was able to pass through the region to which he had been peculiarly vulnerable without any manifestations.

Another scientific acquaintance had a bothersome skin condition until he discovered that large doses of vitamin A (10 times the recommended daily allowance) if taken consistently would clear it up. Later, when he was for many months in a foreign country where he could not easily obtain supplies of vitamin A, the condition recurred. He returned to this country but thought he would see if the condition didn't cure itself. Instead it became aggravated. In the end he began taking large doses of vitamin A again, with the result that the condition cleared up. Another physician friend told me of a patient who for quite different reasons needed continuously over a period of years the same high dosage of vitamin A.

It should not be a matter of surprise, in view of our previous discussion, that a nutritional lack can cause difficulty *in any part of the body.* Nutrition is continuously essential at the cellular level, and whenever cells become deficient trouble results. The trouble can occur wherever cells exist, and of course they are omnipresent in our bodies.

Individual experiences such as we have mentioned are not taken very seriously by scientists who are unaware of the biochemical individuality we discussed in Chapter VI. They say that these results are not "statistically significant." Actually they are not statistically significant with respect to an entire human population, but they may be highly significant for an individual—he may have done the same experiment on himself enough times so as to rule out the reasonable possibility of accident, and his physical well-being is of supreme importance to himself. If the facts of biochemical individuality are as indicated in our earlier discussion, it is essential that we no longer limit our thinking in the field of health to ideas that are statistically significant for the population as a whole. Alcoholism, for example, is not a disease of humanity as a whole; it applies only to some individuals.

Genetotrophic difficulties have been observed in connection with the feeding of animals as well as humans. Dental caries can be induced in rats by improper diets; however, the "improper diets" do not affect rats equally by any means. Certain individual rats may get severe tooth decay when the diet is such as to protect most rats in the colony. On the other hand when the diet is such as to promote severe tooth decay in most rats in the colony, some rats will be completely protected. Similar results have been obtained in connection with nutritionally induced perosis (slipped-tendon disease) in chickens. A diet which may completely protect most of the fowls in the flock may cause relatively severe perosis in 1 or 2 per cent —the individual fowls which have relatively high requirements for the crucial element (manganese).

It is found that when cattle are allowed to graze on wheat a certain few develop "wheat disease" (a paralytic condition) and that these particular animals are not getting enough calcium. When calcium is administered, the paralysis disappears. The other cattle in the herd—eating the very same diet—get enough calcium; evidently their requirements are not so high. A similar condition exhibited by a few animals under different circumstances is known as "grass disease," which seems to be due to a high requirement for magnesium.

It thus appears evident that the genetotrophic concept has diverse applications. If, for genetic reasons, a person is susceptible to a particular disease, this need not spell his doom. Wise adjustment of nutrition may make possible a complete avoidance of the disease.

The genetotrophic concept places a very high importance upon nutrition. That nutrition is of utmost importance should not occasion surprise when we remember the logic behind the adage "we are what we eat." The reason we have not been able to get the most out of nutritional science is that we have not been able to apply it on an individual basis. We have neglected inborn differences.

On the basis of modern genetics there is excellent reason to think that every individual, from the time of the fertilization of the egg, brings with him a nutritional problem which, to a degree, is unique. Like other human beings he needs potassium, iron, tryptophane, pantothenic acid, ascorbic acid, and many other elements. But the *amounts* needed are distinctive in each case. If one's needs are modest and are easily met one has an "excellent constitution" and may remain well and disease-resistant all his life, without any particular attention to the quality or quantity of his food. If on the other hand his needs are exacting and not easily met he may have great difficulty in feeding himself in such a way as to maintain health.

There is a possibility that some individuals have a high requirement for some undiscovered nutritional component. In this case it is not likely that the individual can get help until further facts are discovered. The day will come when physicians will be able to test their patients for specific needs, but the tools for doing this are not well developed, and will not be adequate until more attention is paid to individuality in nutrition. Fortunately some treatments can be devised which do not require preliminary study of each individual patient. In a following chapter we will give at least the first portion of a brief history of how the genetotrophic idea has been applied to the treatment of alcoholism.

We have been very much interested in the genetotrophic concept because it points the way toward a practical environmental method of controlling alcoholism. As we have previously indicated, it seems inconceivable that biochemical individuality should be a negligible factor in this disease. It is conceivable that some other means such as direct hormone administration, or even surgery, may be found to be another way of accomplishing the same purpose. The distinctive endocrine systems of individuals have been studied almost not at all, and endocrinology as a branch of science is far less advanced than nutrition. It seems extremely doubtful whether any known hormonal procedure can yield anything like uniform or dependable results. The nutritional approach seems a logical one, in view of its extraordinary success in some cases and in view of the fact that if an ailing body is supplied with the right nutritional elements it may be able to make and secrete its own hormones. In the normal scheme of nature, nutrition is supplied from without our bodies, hormones are produced within, that is, endogenously.

VIII. Alcohol Consumption by Experimental Animals

$\mathbb{I}$T WOULD BE DIFFICULT to exaggerate the importance of animal experimentation in the development of knowledge regarding human ailments. So much that we know about anatomy, physiology, biochemistry, pharmacology, and nutrition is derived initially from animal experimentation, that we are never surprised when new insights come from this source. The results of animal experiments cannot always be interpreted directly in human terms, but they are always suggestive and often are fully corroborated later by human experience.

A study of alcohol consumption by experimental animals (principally rats and, to a minor extent, mice) has led us into the development of a number of the ideas regarding alcoholism which are being presented in this book.

When we place experimental rats in separate cages and give them two bottles from which to drink—one containing 10 per cent alcohol and the other water— we are in position to test their physiological urge to drink, to determine whether it is based upon a liking for the taste, or upon a more deep-seated bodily craving. In the case of rats one may safely discount, at least as a first approximation, any psychological desire to escape from their troubles or any social pressure. By alternating the positions of the drinking bottles one can eliminate the factor that animals may get into the habit of drinking from a particular position.

In our laboratories we have carried out thousands of experiments of this kind on rats; a description of these, in detail, would require several books.[1] So we must be content with a summary of our findings,

[1] Roger J. Williams, L. J. Berry, and E. Beerstecher, Jr., "Individual Metabolic Patterns, Alcoholism, Genetotrophic Diseases," *Proceedings of the National Academy of Sciences U.S.*, Vol. 35, No. 6 (1949), pp. 265–271; "Biochemical Individuality—III. Genetotrophic Factors in the Etiology of Alcoholism," *Archives of Biochemistry*, Vol. 23, No. 2 (1949), pp. 275–290; "Genetotrophic Diseases: Alcoholism," *Texas Reports on Biology and Medicine*, Vol. 8, No. 2 (1950), pp. 238–256; E. Beerstecher, Jr., J. G. Reed, W. D. Brown,

which, fortunately, are clear-cut and fully convincing so far as they go. For these studies, we have used mostly white rats (sometimes piebald strains) such as are commonly used for nutritional and other experiments.

The first important finding is that such rats exhibit a high degree of *individuality* in their behavior when they are all fed alike and treated alike in every way. This individuality encompasses the whole biochemical realm as is evidenced, for example, by the fact that each rat has a distinctive excretion pattern, but we are interested now primarily in their drinking behavior. When treated in a standard way and fed a standard stock diet, some rats will refuse to drink any alcohol even though it is in front of their noses and must be rejected every day for months. Others will drink a little —but very little—continuously for months. Still others will drink a little at first, but in several weeks their drinking is at a fairly high level. Others speed up their drinking so that even though they start at a low level, they may be up to a high level of consumption in about

and L. J. Berry, "The Effects of Single Vitamin Deficiencies on the Consumption of Alcohol by White Rats," *The University of Texas Publication 5109* (1951), p. 115.

J. G. Reed, "Individual Excretion Patterns in Laboratory Rats," *The University of Texas Publication 5109* (1951), p. 139; "A Study of the Alcoholic Consumption and Amino Acid Excretion Patterns of Rats of Different Inbred Strains," *The University of Texas Publication 5109* (1951), p. 144.

Roger J. Williams, R. B. Pelton, and L. L. Rogers, "Dietary Deficiencies in Animals in Relation to Voluntary Alcohol and Sugar Consumption," *Quarterly Journal of Studies on Alcohol*, Vol. 16, No. 2 (1955), pp. 234–244.

two weeks. Still other rats will drink alcohol at fairly high levels at the start and will continue to drink as long as it is offered to them. Some rats appear to behave something like periodic drinkers in that they may drink heavily for a day or two and then abstain for several days before partaking again.

It would be a mistake, I believe, to say that some are afflicted with "alcoholism" in the sense that humans are. They do not ordinarily show intoxication nor are they, from the human point of view, incapacitated for the "duties" associated with their encaged lives. They often possess a physiological urge to drink alcohol, however, and it is important, and fortunate, that we have a means of studying and modifying this physiological urge. The results of such modifications have been highly suggestive, and since they have been duplicated hundreds of times, there is no doubt of their significance.

This individuality in drinking patterns of the rats goes even further than we have indicated. We have been able to modify the drinking patterns of many of the rats by methods which will be discussed shortly, but we find great variations in the success that we have in changing the pattern. Some rats which drink heavily are relatively resistant to modification in the direction of less consumption. Some other heavy drinkers respond immediately and completely. Some rats which are "teetotalers" resist change in the direction of "taking a little drink," while other "teetotalers" exhibit less resistance.

Our second finding is that this individuality in drinking behavior as well as in excretion patterns, is genetically determined. Several closely inbred strains of rats have been studied extensively, both with respect to their drinking behavior and their excretion patterns. Each strain has its own characteristics both with respect to drinking behavior and excretion patterns. There are some substantial variations within each strain, but the extensive evidence goes to show that two animals with exactly the same genetic background (and fed the same diet) will exhibit substantially the same drinking behavior, and the same excretion patterns. The exhibition of a physiological urge to drink alcohol is, in rats, based upon their inheritance.

A third finding from the animal experiments is just as definite and conclusive as the first two and in some respects more interesting—what the rats have to eat, that is, the chemical composition of their food, is a potent factor in determining how great is their physiological urge to drink alcohol. In scores of cases we have been able to show that a rat's urge to drink is abolished by giving it a missing food element.

Rats that drink heavily on a standard stock ration, which, however, is not necessarily perfect, may stop drinking overnight when the ration is fortified with needed extra vitamins. Repeatedly rats have been made deficient with respect to a specific vitamin (e.g., thiamin, riboflavin, pantothenic acid, pyridoxine) with the result that their alcohol consumption climbs up to five, ten, or twenty times the original level. Immediately on supplying the missing vitamin the alcohol consumption drops again to the original level or even below. In one experiment of nearly eight months' duration a rat was made deficient three separate times. Its alcohol consumption rose to about thirty times its minimum consumption, then dropped in a few days to almost nothing when it was given a single dose of the missing vitamins. The consumption rose again to a high level after a few weeks as the animal gradually became deficient, but consumption stopped when it was given a single dose of missing vitamins as before. Again it became deficient after about sixty days on the marginal diet and its drinking was again at a high level. It was given a series of doses of the missing vitamins and its alcohol consumption dropped to lower than ever and remained there until the experiment was terminated six weeks later.

There is no question whatever that the tendency of experimental animals to drink alcohol is influenced most remarkably by the composition of the food that they get.

How does a deficient diet promote alcohol consumption in rats? We have already indicated that rats can have their wisdom of the body impaired by malnutrition and that as a result they will consume more sugar. It appears that the same type of mechanism is involved with respect to alcohol consumption. The appetite-control mechanisms of the brains of rats need complete and fully adequate nutrition just as do all organs and tissue in the rat's body. When these mechanisms are malnourished, they, in the language of slang, go "haywire." Body wisdom becomes body foolishness, and instead of promoting a craving for good food (which the rat needs) the deranged mechanisms promote the urge to drink alcohol, which in turn increases the deficiency.

An important fact pertinent to this discussion needs to be fully recognized. A particular rat (or human being) consumes day after day approximately a given quota of calories. If some of these calories are consumed in the form of alcohol, this prevents the consumption of a like quantity of well-balanced food which should contain amino acids, minerals, and vitamins (none of which alcohol contains).

The situation is comparable to that which is involved in lubricating an outboard motor or similar engine in which the fuel and the lubricant may be mixed together. One uses normally in an outboard motor a fixed proportion of fuel and lubricant, and let us say that all goes well. If one pours a small amount of straight gasoline into the fuel tank, no great harm is done. If, however, one substitutes straight gasoline for a large part of the fuel-lubricant mixture, the result will be serious. The machinery will no longer be lubricated and will shortly "go to pieces" and cease to operate. If we attempt to run our bodies simply on fuel, with no "lubricants" (in the form of amino acids, minerals, and vitamins), we are headed for disaster, because without these other food elements our bodies are absolutely incapable of operating continuously.

Another finding we have made with experimental animals is that *stresses and annoyances can increase the physiological urge to drink alcohol.* We have placed flashing lights and jangling cow bells going day and night, near the cages of rats undergoing observation.[2] These stimuli are capable of actually "driving the animals to drink" even when the food was good enough to prevent alcohol consumption under ordinary circumstances. Some "teetotaler" rats who on the stock diet did not drink at all, were induced to drink when they were subjected to these stresses.

In other laboratories it has been found that rats subjected to stress may have their requirements for certain food elements materially increased. The need of rats for pantothenic acid, for example, is increased by stressful treatments.[3] This being the case, it is obvious that stress can cause nutritional deficiency, and it may easily be that it is the nutritional deficiency (operating to impair the healthy condition of the appetite-controlling mechanisms) which causes the physiological urge to drink alcohol, rather than the direct effect of stress itself.

We cannot emphasize too strongly the fact that individual experimental animals having somewhat different ancestry, behave very differently with respect to alcohol consumption. Uniformly they exhibit a

[2] Unpublished findings, University of Texas Clayton Foundation Biochemical Institute.

[3] M. E. Dumm and E. P. Ralli, "Influence of Pantothenic Acid on Response of Adrenalectomized and Intact Rats to Stress," *Federation Proceedings,* Vol. 9, No. 1 (1950), p. 34.

physiological urge to drink when their diets are made deficient, but deficiency for one animal may be very different from deficiency for another. Some animals are very easily made deficient; others can tolerate what we regard as marginal diets very well by comparison.

When animals are on a standard stock diet, some exhibit deficiency; others do not. When animals which do exhibit deficiency (by relatively heavy consumption of alcohol) have their diets supplemented, they are not uniformly relieved of their deficiency by the administration of *the same* specific vitamins. Some need more of one food element; others need another or a combination of several. The biochemical individuality of the animals is clearly in evidence.

In recent years we have been breeding a strain of rats that are relatively difficult to handle from the standpoint of curtailing their alcohol consumption. It is difficult to fortify their diets so that they have no physiological urge to drink. We believe that there are nutritional factors as yet unrecognized (undiscovered vitamins possibly) which if given in abundance to these rats (in addition to everything else they need) would cause them to lose their urge to drink.

It is a well-known principle that in the field of nutrition a chain is as strong as its weakest link. Let us assume for the moment that our bodies need approximately forty food elements (this is about the right number) and that one of the forty is present in the diet at too low a level. The result is malnutrition just as certainly as it would be if the diet were deficient in ten different items!

This same principle holds for the nutrition of the hypothalamus and of the other tissues which regulate food—and drink—consumption. If they lack any single thing, they are malnourished. This principle, coupled with the undeniable facts of biochemical individuality, seems to be fully borne out by our investigation. Animals can be deficient in any one of a number of different food elements. The result—malnutrition and malfunctioning of the appetite-controlling centers—is the same. Body wisdom is transformed to body foolishness.

IX. The Genetotrophic Idea
and Alcoholism

ALTHOUGH THE APPLICATION of the genetotrophic principle to the treatment of alcoholism has not been accepted even on a trial basis by the medical profession, many physicians have collaborated with us in connection with our cases and many others have a keen interest.

The reasons for general reticence are understandable—often they are very human reasons—especially so because the genetotrophic idea is a new and revolutionary one, and alcoholism has come to be considered as in the domain of psychiatrists, many of whom could not be expected, because of the psychoanalytic flavor of their background, to be enthusiastic about biochemical and physiological approaches.

Our first advice to alcoholics as set forth in an earlier volume[1] was that they "eat good nourishing foods, including high quality proteins (meats), dairy products, vegetables, fruits in accordance with best nutritional knowledge. The diet ideally should also include one tablespoonful of corn oil (Mazola Oil) daily in salad dressing or other form." The application of the genetotrophic idea is by no means simply "vitamin therapy," though we have, for very good reasons, made substantial use of vitamins.

Our second recommendation involved taking capsules containing supplementary nutrients, (Tycopan or Nutricol) three capsules per day with meals the first week, six per day the second week, and nine capsules per day with meals thereafter. From the standpoint of expense it was desirable to cut down on the daily number to be taken indefinitely, but this could not be judged except individually.

Because this suggested treatment was made freely available to physicians and to the public without restrictions, we can only guess from the thousands of

[1] Roger J. Williams, *Nutrition and Alcoholism* (Norman, University of Oklahoma Press, 1951), p. 39.

inquiries and the larger number of books sold, how many have attempted to take advantage of it. Of these there were no doubt many who failed to give nutritional treatment a real trial. Among the first two dozen or so known patients who did follow the directions with some faithfulness, approximately one-half were greatly benefited and a substantial percentage seemed to be completely freed from alcoholism as long as they followed the recommendations—in some cases for a period of several years.

Aside from some personal contacts with alcoholics who have had their alcoholic craving abolished in a convincing manner, we have learned by correspondence of many others. A few of these additional instances will indicate the character of the results.

One woman after *five* years wrote to say, "Nutricol has proved very beneficial to my husband." She went on to say that he now takes four capsules a day and his excesses are in the past.

Another wife wrote: "Two years ago our family doctor gave my husband a prescription for Tycopan. I hope you will be interested to know that it worked a miraculous change in my husband. The alcoholic compulsion seemed to be gone."

A man, himself the sufferer, wrote, "Now I have achieved what I can only describe as a truly miraculous result—I no longer feel any sense of craving or desire."

Another victim: "I am taking three capsules three times a day and since the third or fourth week I have had no desire to indulge my former appetite for whiskey."

Still another victim says: "When taking the capsules on a steady basis I work well, sleep well and think only of food."

A correspondent from outside this country wrote seven years after the publication of my book: ". . . I immediately thought of your wonderful pioneer work in the vitamin and nutritional help for alcoholics. It worked a complete cure for my husband and helped many, many others that I know of."

After sixteen months a wife wrote: "My husband had been drinking about 26oz. of whiskey a day or more for about 10 years . . . and had tried AA without success. He tried Tycopan with immediate success. Within a couple of months he was completely cured and hasn't had a single relapse."

Another woman writing about her husband says: "I would never have believed that vitamins could have helped my husband who has been a periodical drinker for twenty years. . . . Since I have been secretly putting the extra capsule of vitamin in his breakfast (tomato juice) the results are very good."

Another wife wrote: "My husband has been a pretty steady drinker for about fifteen years with the usual bad results. It (the vitamin supplement) has helped so much and made our life so much happier that I felt I should write you and express my sincere thanks."

A victim of the disease wrote: "I have taken so

many bottles of Nutricol that I have lost count but I think I can truthfully say 'I have licked the problem of alcoholism'."

Another sufferer indicated that when he took the capsules "that terrible anxiety and tension and shaking that had been hounding me for weeks began to melt away." A year later he said "I've taken a hundred dollars worth of Tycopan. I've given a lot of it away. I never felt better."

Another victim, who is obviously interested in helping others, wrote: "I have been able to refrain from taking a drink for several months and by this time I have lost all desire. I gave away quite a few thousand of these tablets and all that used them seemed to benefit although the treatment did not turn out to be complete in all cases."

Another alcoholic sufferer wrote: "Everything is fine both at home and at work. I have been very happy and already expecting a promotion in the near future. Thank you so much for allowing me to be an early patient thus giving me the opportunity to rehabilitate myself. Since I am now living a normal and useful life with my health returned, my greatest wish is that the results of your research may be extended to every alcoholic."

A wife of an alcoholic wrote: "My husband was an alcoholic and began taking Tycopan. I will not bother you with details but the change has been wonderful."

Another in a similar vein wrote: "I was seeking a cure for this man and he *is* cured. In a letter received today he says 'I have no nerves whatsoever. I am peaceful and never so calm before in my life.' It is a miracle!'"

An alcoholic of long standing wrote me: "Speaking as one who has been ill for many years and has tried all the so-called cures, it is my firm opinion that your solution to the problem is the only real answer."

In addition to letters from patients, we have had several reports of reasonable success from physicians and others who continuously deal with large numbers of alcoholics.

These excerpts from unsolicited letters of course have little scientific standing and would have none if they were quoted by someone who had a nostrum to sell. Such is not the case here as is made clear on p. 96. These letters are cited because they give some information as to the different types of experience that alcoholics have. These varied experiences in turn may be duplicated by others. By giving alcoholics information as to what they may expect, these statements should be helpful.

Unfortunately such results as these have not been obtained with regularity. This is why it seems so extraordinarily important to me that other research groups join in the attempt to find out how biochemical individuality enters into the problem and how nutrition can help. If nutrition can work such wonders for some, surely it should be able to help all. Factors which have contributed to incomplete success in many instances are (1) lack of persistence, (2) failure to attend to good all-round nutrition, and (3) experimentation with moderate drinking—a practice which is certainly not to be recommended since it introduces into one's system the very agent that alcoholics need to combat.

There are practical difficulties, however, that have prevented victims of alcoholism from getting the most out of our recommendations. One is the cost involved. At regular drugstore prices the cost of nine "Tycopan" capsules per day (each containing appropriate amounts of the supplements) is about $1.00. Though alcoholics in general could afford this if they were cured and brought back into productiveness, they may not *think* they can, especially if they are not at all sure the treatment will work. At mail-order prices essentially the same formula under a different name, "Nutricol," can be obtained for one-half this price. Even this, however, is more than some patients *think* they can afford. Some people tend to be most generous in buying alcoholic beverages, but penurious about buying other things.

A second drawback, which is probably more serious, is the fact that human nature being what it is, people cannot be counted on to take capsules or other "medication" consistently three times a day, day in and day out for months at a time. A study[2] made recently, in which it was possible to check, has shown that it is exceptional for patients to follow such direc-

[2] B. W. Jenkins, "Are Patients True to t.i.d. and q.i.d. Doses?" *GP*, Kansas City, Vol. 9, No. 6 (1954), pp. 66–69.

tions, and that the majority do not do so even for short periods with reasonable regularity. In the study referred to covering a short period, only 4 out of a group of 22 patients *(all selected for their punctuality and dependability)* took the prescribed medication three times a day. The other 18 were 60 per cent faithful *or less*. The physician making this investigation states that three doses a day is about two doses too many for most people to take faithfully. It is obvious that the more complicated the regimen the less likely it is that it will be followed.

There is, of course, nothing *impossible* about following these suggestions. Alcoholics taken as a group probably would be less systematic and conscientious in following directions than the average of the population, but if an alcoholic with the cooperation of his family wants badly enough to overcome his difficulty, he can follow directions. We shall have more to say about this later. Unfortunately, in a substantial number of alcoholics there is weakened determination; this, together with the lurking attractiveness of excessive alcohol consumption and a lack of a strong and deep desire to be rid of the affliction, may result in failure.

A third obstacle in following the regimen—this is probably minor—is that a few individuals are mildly upset when they suddenly begin using the nutritional supplement; there is something about their body chemistries which requires a gradual acceptance of the program.

There are also very great difficulties that stand in the way of testing out adequately with large groups of alcoholics such a treatment as we have suggested. The only serious attempt which has been reported in full is that of Trulson, Fleming, and Stare described in the *Journal of the American Medical Association* in May, 1954.[3] The "summary and conclusions" of their study is given in full as follows:

While the results of the treatment of alcoholism by means of dietary supplements were somewhat disappointing on a group basis, there is evidence that a number of patients were benefited. Of the 32 alcoholic patients who took part in the nutritional study for 13 months or more, 25 had vitamin medication and 7 continued with placebos[blanks]. Of those taking vitamins, seven patients were abstinent, seven were controlled, two were improved, and nine exhibited no change, while, of those taking the placebos, one was abstinent, and six exhibited no change. The fact that the number of patients taking vitamins was larger than the number taking placebos was because many of the patients were in such extreme circumstances that placebo therapy was not justified.

There is evidence that not all the patients took the medication prescribed, and this factor inevitably operates to diminish the apparent effectiveness of the treatment. The results of this study do not suggest optimism with respect to widespread benefits to be derived from presently available vitamin medication; it does, however, indicate that some persons

[3] M. F. Trulson, R. Fleming, and F. J. Stare, "Vitamin Medication in Alcoholism," *The Journal of the American Medical Association,* Vol. 155, No. 2 (1954), pp. 114–119.

are benefited by vitamin therapy. The results are sufficiently favorable to warrant additional research on the effects of nutritional supplements in the treatment and on the metabolism of alcohol.

It will be noted that the authors call attention to the failure of some of the patients to take the medication and that this failure operates to make the treatment appear less successful than it would otherwise. In a case like this where some of the patients were being given placebos and the results of the proposed treatment were unknown, it would have been impossible for the physicians or others to carry conviction to their patients regarding the importance of taking of the capsules regularly. Furthermore, instead of using one capsule in which all the supplements were combined, *five kinds* of capsules or tablets were administered. In view of all of these facts it is probably a generous estimate to say that one-third of the patients who were supposed to be taking the supplements *actually took them* with reasonable regularity. When this is considered the results thereby become much more impressive. Even so because of the nature of the experiment, it was impossible to give the whole nutritional idea a fair trial by giving *no nutritional advice* to those receiving placebos, and *full advice* and instructions to those receiving medication.

In my extensive correspondence and discussions with many victims of alcoholism, the slap-dash attitude toward nutrition and nutritional supplements often encountered is sometimes discouraging. Some think that if they take a few "vitamin pills" (most any kind) occasionally, they have given our ideas a trial, whereas, of course, they haven't at all. Too few of those who have "tried" Tycopan or Nutricol have given these supplements a satisfactory trial even for a limited period. In a fair test it is necessary to take nutritional supplements *regularly in sufficient amounts, and for extended periods of time.* Nutritional supplementation is a serious project and must be undertaken with diligence and carried along for months before it can be called a real trial.

Another practical difficulty in helping alcoholics is inherent in the disease itself. Alcoholics in their diseased condition have too often taken the attitude of wanting *help.* But help of what kind? Help so they can drink safely. This usually means heavy drinking, because this is the only kind they know. At no time have I felt that this kind of help could be given or that it was desirable for it to be given. In spite of any advice which my associates or I have given, some alcoholics have been determined to experiment with themselves to see if they can drink. If they find they can drink a little with apparent safety, then they try to drink more, with the result that they may eventually be back again in the category of the alcoholic. On mature consideration it is my opinion that recognized alcoholics as a group should follow the principle to which Alcoholics Anonymous adhere. They should become total abstainers. When wise eating, coupled with nutritional supplements, makes it possible for them to abstain, they should strive valiantly to find other things in life worth living for. Good nutrition should help them think straight in connection with this endeavor.

Before discussing some of the newer findings with respect to the application of the genetotrophic principle to alcoholism, we wish to call attention to some of the side effects which have been observed when individuals have taken the recommended nutritional supplements referred to above. Some individuals have been relieved of headaches as a result of the nutritional supplements; others who previously suffered from insomnia have had the trouble banished; one was greatly improved in his muscular coordination and sense of balance; some have had their high blood pressure brought down to normal; at least one has lost his dependence on high doses of barbiturates; one found he could tolerate coffee without a previous alcoholic drink; one found immediate relief from excessively perspiring (and malodorous) feet; some have ceased to have trouble with constipation; many have gained substantial relief from hay fever manifestations.

All of these have been unlooked-for benefits, and hence were not the result of any previous "suggestion." In the light of what we have had to say about the importance of cellular nutrition, these findings should not be too surprising. Body cells were involved in every one of these difficulties, and in each case it appears that nutrition was at fault, and was corrected. How far corrected nutrition (with the use of supplements) can go in the curing of miscellaneous ills is yet to be demonstrated, but certainly our findings hold out hope with respect to this possibility. Biochemical individuality, that is, the differences in the body chemistry of individuals, must, however, be continuously taken into account.

For those who are skeptical about the possibilities of dramatic achievements through nutrition in the control of such a disease as alcoholism (which is often regarded as a "mental" disease), let us consider what one of the vitamins has done in the case of another disease, which has far more marked mental symptoms than does alcoholism. A woman patient thought her neighbors were conspiring to kill her; she often had imaginary violent encounters with various vicious animals—not only could she see them; she could *feel* their attacks. Eventually she became unmanageable and paid no attention whatever to conversation or to the doctor's instructions. It would take no expert to know that she was "of unsound mind." She was given a nutritional supplement and in forty-eight hours was completely cured of her mental derangement. She could then talk and act rationally; she could remember that she had been "crazy" and was greatly relieved to know that her craziness was now in the past. Everything made sense now, and in a few days she could go back to her home to perform the duties of a housewife free from the devastating suspicions and imaginings.

The condition from which she was suffering was primarily a deficiency of niacin, one of the B vitamins contained in our recommended food supplement. If our food supplement had been available at the time and had been administered it would have yielded the dramatic results described. The fact that the condition is known as pellagra and is now recognized as due to malnutrition does not alter the findings as outlined. Other sufferers from this deficiency have received similar benefits,[4] and there is no doubt that nutritional supplementation in these cases is capable of revolutionizing one's thinking and acting.

The potential value of nutritional supplements is not ruled out, even if we regard alcoholism as a mental disease. It is widely known that if you can keep an alcoholic sober (and eating) a few days, many of his psychological troubles will melt away. Alcoholism is somewhat more complex than pellagra in that many different deficiencies can contribute to its severity, and, because of the biochemical individuality we have discussed earlier, it is not easy to point out in any individual where the seat of his particular biochemical difficulty lies. When the particular deficiency from which an individual is suffering is abolished by supplementation the results have been magnificently successful. We need eventually through extensive research in a number of laboratories to be able to do the same for every individual.

I have often been asked whether nutrition can be

[4] H. M. Cleckley, V. P. Sydenstricker, and L. E. Geeslin, "Nicotinic Acid in the Treatment of Atypical Psychotic States Associated with Malnutrition," *The Journal of the American Medical Association,* Vol. 112, No. 21 (1939), p. 2107; Karl M. Bowman and Herman Wortis, "Psychiatric Syndromes Caused by Nutritional Deficiency,"

expected to play a role in drug addiction similar to that which it plays in alcoholism.

It seems probable that poisoning by morphine and its derivatives is so severe and so difficult to recover from that violent withdrawal symptoms are almost inescapable. It seems reasonable to suppose that any addict who is "off" the drug will stand a better chance of staying off, if his nutrition is optimal. It is well recognized in addiction centers that in barbiturate addicts poor nutrition fosters severe withdrawal symptoms and other difficulties whereas good nutrition tends to abolish these difficulties. Furthermore in Bolivia and Peru where Indians are often addicted to the chewing of coca leaves, it has been found that this addiction can be overcome without difficulty *provided the victims are placed on well balanced diets.*

There are many areas in which the potentialities of nutrition (taking genetics into account) need to be further explored.

The Role of Nutritional Deficiency in Nervous and Mental Disease (Proceedings of the Association for Research in Nervous and Mental Disease, XXII (1943), 178).

X. Improved Food Supplements
—Glutamine

CONSISTENTLY IN PAST YEARS in our discussions of the use of nutritional supplements for the treatment of alcoholism, we have pointed out the imperfectness of our present knowledge and have stressed the hope that in the future, with increased knowledge, better nutritional supplements can be devised.

The food supplements which we originally recommended to be taken in addition to good food included one tablespoon of corn oil (Mazola) in salad dressing and capsules containing the following ingredients:

Thiamine	3.30 mg.
Riboflavin	2.67 mg.
Nicotinamide	10.00 mg.
Calcium pantothenate	10.00 mg.
Pyridoxin	3.30 mg.
Biotin	0.05 mg.
Folic acid	1.10 mg.
p-Aminobenzoic acid	11.00 mg.
Inositol	53.00 mg.
Choline	53.00 mg.
Vitamin B_{12}	5.00 μg.
Vitamin A	6,667.00 units
Vitamin C	33.30 mg.
α-Tocopherol	6.67 mg.
Viosterol	333.00 units

There are now four specific lines of potential improvement which need to be considered. The first but not necessarily the most important of these has to do with minerals. We have not made extensive trials with experimental animals to learn whether mineral deficiencies could produce alcoholic craving. Such experiments as we have done have not pointed to minerals as crucially important, and for this reason no minerals were included originally in our recommended supplement.

Mineral supply could theoretically be at fault, however, and the expense of mineral supplementation is inherently so small that the inclusion of a suitable assortment of trace minerals is worthy of consideration. We have studied this problem[1] and suggest the following as suitable "unit dosages": manganese, 5 mg.; iron, 10 mg.; copper, 2 mg.; cobalt, 0.05 mg.; zinc, 5 mg.; iodide, 0.05 mg.; molybdenum, 0.2 mg. These "unit dosages" approximate the average daily needs and a maximum of six "unit dosages" may be recommended daily in a trial supplement. How much such a supplement would contribute to the alleviation of the physiological craving for alcohol is not yet determined, but there is at least a small probability that it will make the supplement more complete for some individuals. How many might be helped, no one knows.

Another source of potential improvement of the nutritional supplement is a new vitamin, lipoic acid (thioctic acid), which was first isolated chemically by my associate Dr. Lester Reed.[2] This has three things in its favor. First, it is a newly discovered vitamin and has been found under some conditions to promote the growth and well-being of certain strains of rats (and chickens) when added to the diet in tiny amounts.[3]

[1] Roger J. Williams and L. L. Rogers, "The Formulation of a Genetotrophic Supplement for the Experimental Treatment of Diseases of Obscure Etiology," *Texas Reports on Biology and Medicine,* Vol. 11, No. 3 (1953), pp. 573–581.

[2] L. J. Reed, "The Chemistry and Function of Lipoic Acid," *Advances in Enzymology,* XVIII (1957), 319–347.

[3] B. G. DeBusk and Roger J. Williams, "Effect of Lipoic Acid on the Growth Rate of Young Chicks and Rats," *Archives of Biochemistry and Biophysics,* Vol. 55, No. 2 (1955), pp. 587–588.

The fact that these results are not obtained with consistency is a puzzler, but it does not cancel out the statistically significant positive results that have been obtained. One part of lipoic acid per million parts of dry food was found to be enough to benefit certain animals materially. Secondly, lipoic acid has been synthesized by Dr. Reed and others and should be cheap enough so that the expense of including it in the supplement should be very small. Thirdly, and more important, lipoic acid administration has been found by investigators in Chile[4] to diminish alcohol consumption in experimental animals. According to these workers, at least, it is one of the looked-for and missing vitamins needed to control alcohol consumption by experimental rats.

There is more than a slim probability that including lipoic acid will improve the nutritional supplement which we have devised, and the amount which we suggest is 0.1 mg. per capsule. This may be increased as price levels decrease.

The third improvement of our nutritional supplement involves doubling the amount of three already recognized vitamins, nicotinamide, pantothenic acid (B_3) and ascorbic acid (vitamin C).

The increase in the amount of nicotinamide (niacin-

[4] J. Mardones, N. Segovia, A. Hederra, and F. Alcaino, "Influence of Sulfasuxidine on the Effect of Alpha Lipoic or Thioctic Acid on the Voluntary Intake of Rats Depleted of Factor N.," *Acta Physiologica Lationamericana*, 3(2/3) (1953), pp. 140–143; "Effect of Synthetic Thioctic or Alpha Lipoic Acid on the Voluntary Alcohol Intake of Rats," *Science*, Vol. 119 (1954), pp. 735–736.

amide) is based largely upon the findings of Kaufman[5] to the effect that in some cases individuals are bene-fited by amounts of this vitamin far in excess of what is usually administered. Large amounts even (1 gram per day) appear to be quite harmless.

The need for an increase in the pantothenic-acid level is indicated because in recent years an increasing amount of evidence has accumulated that human pan-tothenic-acid deficiencies exist, and since it is needed in the normal metabolism of alcohol, there is a good chance that this may be a weak link in the nutrition of many individuals. A factor which may contribute to this deficiency is the extensive toasting of various foods, breads, breakfast foods, etc. Dry heat destroys pantothenic acid rapidly and enriched bread or flour or breakfast cereals do not at present have any supple-mentary pantothenic acid added. A further reason for increasing the level of pantothenic acid is an informal report from Great Britain that it has been found to be an important factor in using vitamin therapy on alco-holics. The doubling of the pantothenic acid may turn out to be the most important change we have made. Pantothenic acid, even at extremely high levels, is harmless.

The increase in the ascorbic acid level is made on the basis that its level, by ordinary standards, is too low. Drs. Trulson, Stare, and Fleming[6] used an in-

[5] William Kaufman, *The Common Form of Joint Dysfunction* (Brattleboro, Vermont, E. L. Hildreth and Co., 1949).

[6] M. F. Trulson, R. Fleming, and F. J. Stare, "Vitamin Medication

creased level in their experiments. While we have no direct evidence that vitamin C plays an important role in alcoholism, it nevertheless may do so directly or indirectly.

Our complete recommended vitamin supplement therefore contains the following items in each "unit dosage." The number of "unit dosages" to be taken is from three to nine daily depending on the individual case and the stage in the treatment.

Thiamine (B_1)	3.30	mg.
Riboflavin (B_2)	2.67	mg.
Nicotinamide	20.00	mg.
Calcium pantothenate (B_3)	20.00	mg.
Pyridoxin	3.30	mg.
Biotin	0.05	mg.
Folic acid	1.10	mg.
p-Aminobenzoic acid	11.00	mg.
Inositol	53.00	mg.
Choline	53.00	mg.
Vitamin B_{12}	5.00	μg.
Vitamin A	6,667.00	units
Vitamin C	66.70	mg.
α-Tocopherol	6.67	mg.
Viosterol	333.00	units
Lipoic acid	0.10	mg.

The fourth development belongs in a separate category and is of unusual importance. Its discovery is due to the pioneering investigations of my colleague and

in Alcoholism," *The Journal of the American Medical Association,* Vol. 155, No. 2 (1954), pp. 114–119.

associate, Dr. William Shive. It occurred to him that in studying the effects of alcohol on organisms it would be interesting to see if microorganisms could not be utilized. He found actually that there was an unknown substance in natural extracts which protected bacteria to a substantial degree against the poisoning effects of alcohol. Bacterial cells require nutrition just as other cells do, and it appeared that giving certain bacterial cells this additional "unknown" caused them to be healthier and to withstand much better the introduction of alcohol in their environment.

The second chapter in the story of this development was the chemical isolation of this unknown by Dr. Shive and his associates.[7] It turned out to be *glutamine,* an easily decomposed amino acid found in proteins, which has hitherto been thought nonessential for animal nutrition. This pure substance in small amounts counteracted to a marked degree the poisonous effect of alcohol for the bacteria he used in his study.

The next chapter in the story of glutamine is the finding made in our laboratories that administering glutamine to experimental rats diminishes materially their physiological urge to drink alcohol.[8] This ques-

[7] J. M. Ravel, B. Felsing, E. M. Lansford, Jr., R. H. Trubey, and W. Shive, "Reversal of Alcohol Toxicity by Glutamine," *The Journal of Biological Chemistry,* Vol. 214, No. 2 (1955), pp. 497–501.

[8] L. L. Rogers, R. B. Pelton, and Roger J. Williams, "Voluntary Alcohol Consumption by Rats Following Administration of Glutamine," *The Journal of Biological Chemistry,* Vol. 214, No. 2 (1955), pp. 503–506; "Amino Acid Supplementation and Voluntary Alcohol Consumption by Rats," *The Journal of Biological Chemistry,* Vol. 220, No. 1 (1956), pp. 321–323.

tion has been studied carefully and the significant effect of glutamine cannot be questioned. It has been compared with its chemical relatives glutamic acid, asparagin, and the simpler amino acid glycine. These other substances had no effect whatever, but glutamine consistently decreased alcohol consumption. It must furnish a nutritional link not hitherto recognized, thus contributing to the well-being of the cells, in the hypothalamus or elsewhere in the nervous system of the rats, which control alcohol consumption. It is entirely possible that in some rats these cells are more vulnerable to alcohol poisoning than in others and that the addition of this particular boost in their nutrition helps them resist this poisoning.

The final chapter in the glutamine story concerns its use on humans. In some alcoholics, remarkable responses have been obtained from using glutamine alone as a nutritional supplement. In one case reported by Dr. J. B. Trunnell in Houston[9] an individual confirmed alcoholic stopped drinking when glutamine was administered daily without the patient's knowledge. In fact the patient did not know that anything was being administered. Rehabilitation and a job resulted, and at last reports two years later the patient was free from alcoholic craving.

This case is not an isolated one. At the same meet-

[9] J. B. Trunnell and J. I. Wheeler, "Preliminary Report on Experiments with Orally Administered Glutamine in Treatment of Alcoholics," a paper presented at the Southwest Regional Meeting of the American Chemical Society, Houston, December, 1955.

ing at which Dr. Trunnell's report was given, my colleague, Dr. Lorene Rogers, cited a number of cases in which glutamine helped alcoholics greatly, whereas placebos were in general without effect.[10] Enough experiments have been made with alcoholics to indicate that the effectiveness of glutamine for some of them is unquestionable. As in our experience with the earlier nutritional supplements it is found that some alcoholics respond less readily. Biochemical individuality is such that different alcoholics may have different nutritional vulnerabilities. They respond differently to different food elements because the pattern of needs for each is distinctive.

Further evidence for the effectiveness of glutamine in alcoholism is the parallel finding that glutamine is important for the nutrition of other parts of the body as well. Excellent evidence has been adduced, for example,[11] that its administration shortens the healing time for ulcers. Promising improvements in the treatment of mentally deficient children have also been recently observed.[12] It is possible that the relatively in-

[10] L. L. Rogers, "Some Biological Effects of Glutamine," a paper presented at the Southwest Regional Meeting of the American Chemical Society, Houston, December, 1955; L. L. Rogers and R. B. Pelton, "Glutamine in the Treatment of Alcoholism," *Quarterly Journal of Studies on Alcohol,* Vol. 18, No. 4 (1957), pp. 581–587.

[11] W. Shive, R. N. Snider, B. DuBilier, J. C. Rude, G. E. Clark, Jr., and J. O. Ravel, "Glutamine in Treatment of Peptic Ulcer," *Texas State Journal of Medicine,* Vol. 53 (1957), pp. 840–843.

[12] L. L. Rogers and R. B. Pelton, "Effect of Glutamine on IQ Scores of Mentally Deficient Children," *Texas Reports on Biology and Medicine,* Vol. 15, No. 1 (1957), pp. 84–90.

nocent experiments involving the poisoning of bacteria with alcohol may have led to a major medical discovery.

Glutamine has one distinct advantage. It is tasteless (to most, at least) and certainly is harmless in any amounts that are likely to be used. It is a natural food substance which we have known for years to be present in combined form in foods, but it has commonly been thought of as of no particular significance. Because it is a harmless, tasteless food substance, it can, if necessary, be put into a patient's drinking water, for example, without his knowledge.

There is, however, one drawback to the use of glutamine. The amount required is relatively large and the cost is by no means negligible. When our first experiments with humans were made the cost was several dollars for a single dose. The price has decreased to much more reasonable levels, and will undoubtedly decline further when the demand is sufficient to warrant production on a larger scale.

In a later chapter we will make more specific recommendations with respect to the use of glutamine, and other supplements, in the treatment of alcoholism.

There is no question but that in the past five years substantial advance has been made and that our improved supplement will help a larger number of alcoholics. We are in a far better position now to make positive recommendations regarding nutritional supplements than we were five years ago, and we believe that the results will prove themselves.

Improved Food Supplements

We are not at the end of the trail yet; further extensive research into the intricacies of biochemical individuality is necessary, and it is our conviction, based upon past experience, that in a few years from now the ability to treat alcoholism by nutritional supplements will be greatly increased.

XI. What We Now Recommend
for Alcoholics

THIS IS NOT THE PLACE for an extended philosophical discussion, but it seems wise to state here that we believe in general in the moral responsibility of each individual for the conduct of his own life. However, we recognize that the ability to exercise will power is impaired in those who are ill from alcoholism, and we are confident that proper nutrition is necessary if this impairment is to be abolished.

What We Now Recommend for Alcoholics

We recognize the effectiveness of the influences of home, church, Alcoholics Anonymous, and other institutions which help to build character and to enrich the lives of alcoholics, and the desirability of these influences. However, as long as nutrition is seriously impaired these psychological and spiritual influences are needlessly handicapped in the efforts to bring about rehabilitation.

A prime consideration in overcoming alcoholism is that the victim build up his nutrition so that his physical condition will increase his power to abstain from alcoholic consumption. His nutrition is more exacting than that of many of his neighbors (who may "get away" with careless eating) and must be watched accordingly. Because of great biochemical individuality it is not possible to formulate in a cookbook fashion a diet which should be followed rigorously by every alcoholic, but there are certain principles which can serve as a guide.

The diet of an alcoholic should contain plenty of high-quality protein. This is found predominantly in such foods as meat, fish, poultry, eggs, milk, and cheese.[1] While there is no set rule that can be followed universally, it is well be bear in mind the common recommendation that adult males should consume

[1] A special high-protein supplement, "Provimalt" (Humanic Brands, Inc., Summit, New Jersey), has been used with marked benefit for some alcoholics. It has the advantage of being rich in high-quality protein (57%) and also palatable (like malted milk). It must be taken in substantial quantities, e.g., in terms of *ounces* per day, in order to be an effective source of protein.

about 70 grams (2.5 oz.) of protein per day. The amounts of different foods required to get 2.5 oz. of protein, are about as follows: steak—about 1 pound, edible portion (meats often contain 60 per cent–70 per cent water); cheese—10 oz.; eggs— about 10, medium size; milk—about 8 one-half-pint glasses. Many other foods contribute some protein to the diet, and the aggregate of these may be substantial. High-protein foods are in general the more expensive ones.

If an alcoholic gets high-quality proteins from the sources indicated, he will inevitably get also some of the minerals and vitamins that he needs, though not in adequate amounts. Milk and dairy products help to contribute these as do fresh fruits and vegetables. Some vegetables, such as cabbage, broccoli, brussels sprouts, and carrots are of especial value because of their relatively high content of calcium. Yellow vegetables contribute vitamin A in conspicuous quantities. Our previous recommendation of a tablespoon of corn oil per day in the form of salad dressing still holds. This is to furnish certain unsaturated fat acids which are essential for mammalian diets. Some alcoholics have told me that they are sure that this helps them overcome their desire for alcohol.

An alcoholic should avoid all refined foods in order to build up his ailing nutrition. Refined foods furnish little or no minerals, vitamins, or high-quality proteins. Important refined food products which should be held at a *minimum* by alcoholics include sugar (syrups), white rice, spaghettis, and macaronis, and white-flour products (which never have all the vitamins and minerals restored). These refined food materials tend to crowd out of the diet, as does alcohol, many of the food elements that are necessary for rehabilitation. If one leaves alcohol alone and restricts himself to good unrefined food for a reasonable time, the body appetite helps to promote the eating of enough food to furnish these essentials. If refined foods are included, they satisfy the appetite without furnishing the things needed for rehabilitation.

It is a patent fact that alcoholics as a group do not eat well; they do not by any means follow the pattern described in the previous paragraphs. As a result of a long period of neglect and abuse, as well as unusually high needs for certain nutritional items, they require nutritional rehabilitation. It is for this reason we recommend *in addition to good food,* the supplement formulated on p. 86. This supplement unfortunately does not furnish *everything* that may be needed for rehabilitation; it furnishes only certain substances (principally vitamins) which can be supplied in sufficient quantities in capsule form. If we attempted to supply every possible deficiency item in a supplement, the package would be very large, the material might not be very appetizing and the cost would be entirely prohibitive. This is why it is called a food *supplement,* and why eating the right kind of food is so important.

The original food supplement (p. 82) is recommended until the new supplement becomes available. This has been marketed by Eli Lilly and Company under the name "Tycopan," and was available at most drugstores at a cost of about $11.00 per hundred. The same supplement, under the name "Nutricol," has been obtainable at mail-order prices from Vitamin-Quota, 1125 Crenshaw Boulevard, Los Angeles 19, California, or 880 Broadway at Nineteenth, New York 3, New York.

The improved vitamin supplement should be available soon, if not immediately, from the sources indicated above, as well as others. It has been formulated on p. 86.

The writer receives no revenue from the sale of any brand of supplement (the information regarding it has been made public) and has not and will not collect one dollar of revenue from the sale of books dealing with this disease.[2] Any reputable firm may by applying in writing obtain permission, without fee, to market this supplement and to use the writer's name in connection with it, provided acceptable assurances are made so that there will be no abuse. The writer reserves the right to review all such formulations before they are offered for sale and all advertising before it is released.

This food supplement containing vitamins has been worked out carefully, partly on the basis of information gained in our own laboratories on the composition

---

[2] The entire royalties from the present volume will go to the National Council on Alcoholism, Inc., Mrs. Marty Mann, Executive Director, New York Academy of Medicine Building, 2 East 103rd Street, New York.

of human tissues.[3] While we do not regard it as perfect, it is, for the purpose of treating alcoholism, far ahead of the ordinary run of multivitamin preparations put out by the leading drug houses, some of which have formulas which are ridiculously unbalanced. The formulation contains no extract of liver, yeast, alfalfa, or other food material, and advisedly so, since the amounts of these which would have to be used in order to furnish significant amounts of anything of value would be inordinately large. The amounts usually introduced into vitamin supplements are wholly insignificant and have only advertising value.

Unfortunately, because of the biochemical individuality described in Chapter VI, nutritional supplementation must be, to some extent, on a trial-and-error basis. What works for one individual may not be effective for another. What is needed at one stage in the life of an alcoholic may be more than necessary at a later stage. Our suggestion of beginning with three "unit dosages" or capsules per day and building up to nine unit dosages per day within a week or ten days is as good a general recommendation as we can make. If any individual alcoholic finds that abstinence is maintained with nine capsules per day, and he continues to eat highest quality food, it may be possible to cut the supplement back to six, three, or even one capsule per day without impairment of his improved

[3] Alfred Taylor, M. A. Pollack, and R. J. Williams, "B Vitamins in Normal Human Tissues," *The University of Texas Publication 4237* (1942), pp. 41–55.

condition. If he is consistently abstinent over a period of time and his life and associations are such that he can have reasonable hope of remaining so, and if, in addition, he continually watches the quality of his diet, it may be possible for him to abandon the nutritional supplements entirely. Each individual case must be handled separately on the basis of the best judgment available.

An important practical question is: When should the capsules be taken? It is desirable in general to take them with each meal. However, it is a fact that some people are temperamentally unable to follow this pattern. In a study referred to earlier (p. 72) it was found that only a small percentage of more dependable patients actually took prescribed capsules three times a day. In view of this fact our recommendation is that if anyone is inclined to be forgetful and finds it difficult to follow a three-times-a-day pattern, he should take the whole day's supplement at one time, preferably with a heavier meal. It is *vastly more important* for the supplements to be taken *every day,* than it is that they be taken at a specified time of day.

A second supplement which may be used to advantage, as explained in Chapter X, is one containing the following trace minerals:

Manganese	5.00 mg.	Cobalt	0.05 mg.
Iron	10.00 mg.	Zinc	5.00 mg.
Copper	2.00 mg.	Iodine	0.05 mg.
		Molybdenum	0.20 mg.

The use of this supplement is not known to be important. It has not been on the market but may be marketed along with the other nutritional supplement under similar conditions. There are other mineral supplements on the market which may be used. Unfortunately, the fact that they are labelled "mineral supplements" gives no one assurance that they are prepared on an informed or rational basis. Six "unit dosages" or capsules (p. 83) per day is about the maximum that we would recommend and the cost of this amount should not be high. In connection with mineral supplements the large and well-known mail-order houses (in addition to manufacturing pharmaceutical chemists) may well be considered as possible sources.

The recommended use of glutamine to help promote abstinence in alcoholics depends largely upon its availability and upon the results of further experience with it. It is suggested that inquiries be directed to those who market vitamins (rather than to the writer) regarding availability and prices. It can be taken by itself as an adjunct to high quality food; it can also be taken in conjunction with the vitamin supplement or with the vitamin and mineral supplements. We do not have evidence yet as to the preferred procedure. If in an individual case glutamine works wonders when used alone and if it is available at prices that are not prohibitive, the question answers itself.[4] The biochem-

[4] L. L. Rogers and R. B. Pelton, "Glutamine in the Treatment of Alcoholism," *Quarterly Journal of Studies on Alcohol*, Vol. 18, No. 4 (1957), pp. 581–587.

istry of the situation in these instances is such that the vitamin supplement may be capable of doing just what glutamine does (it may actually conserve glutamine or make its production in the body easy), in which case the choice of whether to use glutamine or the vitamin supplement may depend on the cost, convenience, and other factors. It is also possible, however, that glutamine does something for certain individuals which the vitamin supplement will not do; in other words it may be an additional supplement. In such cases the vitamin supplement plus the glutamine supplement will benefit a larger proportion of alcoholics than will either one alone.

The amount of glutamine to be recommended is dependent on such factors as price and availability. On the basis of present knowledge and under prevailing price conditions, the recommended amount is one to two grams per day. More than this would probably be beneficial if the price were not prohibitive. Investigations under way by my colleagues will help to settle this point. It is safe to say that no one is likely to take enough to do the slightest damage, since it is a natural and harmless food substance.

Another recommendation which hitherto has not been made, is that alcoholics, in addition to getting plenty of rest, should seek some kind of regular outdoor or indoor recreation and exercise. Mayer's work[5]

[5] J. Mayer, "The Physiological Basis of Obesity and Leanness," *Nutrition Abstracts and Reviews,* Part I, 25 (1955), 597; Part II, 25 (1955), 871.

clearly indicates that the healthy condition of the appetite center in the brain is promoted by exercise. When our lives grow too sedentary our circulation grows sluggish and we tend to become stagnated. It seems probable that this can cause an increased vulnerability of the appetite-controlling centers in the brain to the poisoning effect of alcohol. While we have no experimental work on which to base a specific prediction, we should be very much surprised if regular exercise (preferably of a recreational nature) would not help any alcoholic to overcome his difficulty.

Just as a tired, stagnant, or hungry body fails to function properly, just so the appetite center of our brain, when impaired by fatigue, lack of circulation, or by inadequate nutrition, fails to do its job well, and thus easily allows itself to become poisoned by alcohol. If not permanently impaired, it should respond to health-restoring measures—rest, good circulation, and fully adequate nutrition—by good performance.

It would take us too far afield if we were to attempt to give advice to alcoholics with regard to cultivating varied interests and to making wise social adjustments. These items are important, and nothing we have had to say indicates the contrary. Anything that promotes the health of the mind promotes the health of the body. This is true, as is also the converse statement that anything which promotes bodily health also promotes a healthy mind.

The author has nothing but admiration for the work of Alcoholics Anonymous. It is his belief that this organization from the beginning has promoted the consumption of good food by getting and keeping alcoholics in a frame of mind in which they can abstain from liquor for shorter or longer periods of time. Consumption of food results from abstinence, and every case is helped nutritionally at least a little; this, as well as the psychological improvement, is a factor in promoting his ability to abstain. Psychological troubles tend to melt away when an alcoholic abstains from liquor and eats good food for a few days. If any member of Alcoholics Anonymous is on the "ragged edge" I would urge him most emphatically to follow the nutritional suggestions given in the previous pages and to give himself a break by using the suggested nutritional supplement at least at the lowest level. I venture that in not fewer than nine cases out of ten he will find it far easier to remain abstinent.

A further fact needs to be brought out. For the sake of alcoholics, those who have no alcoholic difficulties need to be informed and considerate. An informed person knows that it is the essence of bad manners to urge drink upon an individual who is inclined to say no or who has already had enough. The facts of biochemical individuality are highly pertinent here, and the truly considerate and informed individuals will not, by social pressure, seek to curtail the right of each individual to be himself. With respect to the effects of drinking alcoholic liquors, tremendous diversity exists, and should be recognized. It is our opinion that in the great majority of individual alcoholics, the practical elimination of alcoholic craving can be assured, provided the recommendations which we have made are followed. Whether they are followed is a question which must be answered separately in each individual case.

XII. The Prevention of Alcoholism

$\mathbb{B}$EFORE DISCUSSING what we think may be possible in the way of preventing alcoholism, it will be well to clarify a little further what the term "alcoholism" means to us.

One of my well-known medically trained correspondents states his position thus: "My colleagues and I believe that the fundamental basis for an individual to become an alcoholic is an immature personality. While it is true that all immature persons do not become dependent on alcohol to relieve their tensions, we feel strongly that the psychologic make-up of the alcoholic is his principal problem. While this in turn may be basically a biochemical abnormality, that is a long, long way from being established with objective data."

This idea of "immature personality" carries with it the implication that there is such a thing as a "mature personality" toward which we all develop normally. This, I believe, is a serious oversimplification; there are many distinctive types of personalities and there are hundreds of ways in which one may be "immature." At least some careful students of the problem fail to find any personality traits common to all alcoholics.

It is my opinion that in one sense we all have personalities that are imperfect and immature, that is, they fall short of what they might be. That alcoholics have defective personalities I would not deny. It may even be true that they do tend to have distinctive types of personality imperfections. However, personality imperfections have not been classified with sufficient certainty that I, as a scientist, can regard them as very satisfactory reference traits.

It is painfully evident that some alcoholics have defective and "immature" personalities. On the other hand some alcoholics—among them some of the leaders in Alcoholics Anonymous—by any standards that I know, have magnificent personalities. Yet these same individuals with strong personalities are vulnerable (physiologically, I believe) so that a little alcohol can cause disastrous harm.

Whatever can be done socially, religiously, psychologically, or in any other way to help potential alcoholics and others to develop better personalities, this I am in favor of. When it is possible by any of these means to bring alcoholics to the point where they can be substantially free from the grasp of alcoholism, well and good. Many times in the past this has been accomplished through Alcoholics Anonymous.

As set forth in the preface of this book, however, it is abundantly evident that there has been in the past no generally recognized successful medical treatment of the disease. This we believe is largely due to the fact that those who have paid attention to the disease have been so diverted by the rather vague and ill-defined personality disorders that alcoholics allegedly have that they have failed to concentrate upon the one thing that all alcoholics have—whether they are rich or poor, religious or irreligious, brilliant or dull, introverts or extroverts, dominant or submissive, repulsive or charming—namely, *an excessive appetite for alcohol.*

This excessive appetite is what we think nutrition has an excellent chance of preventing. What other results may be concomitant we cannot say. We do not think that good nutrition will guarantee to anyone the possession of a particular type of personality, but we do think it will help prevent the destruction of whatever personality he has by the poisoning effect of alcohol. When we speak of prevention of alcoholism, we refer to the prevention of excessive appetite and the difficulties that result directly from this appetite. We believe that it is in the province of the homes, schools, and churches to build up strong personalities, but that good nutrition is a powerful adjunct which is too often taken for granted and overlooked as an essential factor.

It is our opinion that the disease of alcoholism is *essentially a disease of one's appetite,* and insofar as this is true, it probably can be consistently prevented by the application of nutritional knowledge. The role of individuality in body chemistry must be recognized, as well as the fact that no individual person can be sure, in advance, that he does not have the potentiality of becoming an alcoholic. Any young person who finds himself or herself liking alcohol or its effects very much, or who has any tendency to become intoxicated, should be on his guard.

Alcoholism is such a devastating disease—so real and so prevalent—that it should be possible to educate young people and their parents in the direction of its avoidance. There are few diseases that can bring as much distress into the lives of the victims and their families as can alcoholism, and anyone educated to its perils should, as a matter of course, be willing to put forth some effort to avoid it, especially when there is a special threat.

In many cases it takes several years of relatively heavy drinking to produce an alcoholic. The time to begin precautionary measures is when the heavy drinking starts—not when it has been in progress for some time. I seriously doubt if any except the most extraordinary case would resist treatment if it were begun early rather than late.

The steps in prevention are as follows:

1. Recognition of danger at the latest when heavy drinking *begins*.

2. Extra care in dietary matters, learning the principles of nutrition, and applying them to the individual who is suspected of being vulnerable. Such an individual should follow the dietary precautions set forth as applicable to alcoholics, in the preceding chapter.

3. Use of nutritional supplements in much the same manner as we advise for confirmed alcoholics, except that lower than the maximum levels of intake should suffice.

Recognition of the danger should be possible, and even if the danger should be nonexistent, the individual will never be damaged by eating wisely or taking moderate amounts of nutritional supplements. So, in case there is a threat—too much liking for alcohol, the presence of alcoholism in the family, or the presence of the "earmarks" described below—the potential victim has everything to gain and nothing to lose by taking extra care with his diet.

For several years in our laboratories we have been trying by blood, urine, and saliva analyses to learn what metabolic peculiarities are the accompaniment of alcoholism. A preliminary study indicated that there were certain chemical signs which could be depended on as indicative of alcoholism.[1] This study has been repeated and extended, with the result that there are a number of earmarks which on a statistical basis are characteristic of alcoholic men (who are not drinking at the time) as opposed to nonalcoholic men.[2] The serums of alcoholic men have significantly higher levels of sodium, potassium, and calcium, and the bloods have higher levels of glucose and higher counts of leucocytes, lymphocytes and eosinophils. The urines of alcoholic men are more dilute (lower level of creatinine) and have higher relative levels of hippuric acid, sodium, potassium, and chloride.

Several of these items, while subject to environmental fluctuation, are probably under genetic control[3] and the corresponding biochemical peculiarities probably persist for long periods of time.[4] These tests have not been applied to youngsters sufficiently so that

[1] E. Beerstecher, Jr., H. E. Sutton, H. K. Berry, W. D. Brown, J. Reed, G. B. Rich, L. J. Berry, and Roger J. Williams, "Biochemical Individuality. V. Explorations with Respect to the Metabolic Patterns of Compulsive Drinkers," *Archives of Biochemistry,* Vol. 29, No. 1 (1950), pp. 27–40.

[2] Roger J. Williams, R. B. Pelton, H. M. Hakkinen, and L. L. Rogers, "Identification of Blood Characteristics Common to Alcoholic Males," *Proceedings of the National Academy of Sciences U.S.,* Vol. 44, No. 2 (1958), pp. 216–222.

[3] P. D. Rosahn and A. E. Casey, "Quantitative Variations in the Hemacytologic Constitution of Healthy Men and Rabbits," *American Journal of the Medical Sciences,* Vol. 192, No. 4 (1936), p. 456.

[4] Roger J. Williams, W. D. Brown, and R. W. Shideler, "Metabolic Peculiarities in Normal Young Men as Revealed by Repeated Blood Analyses," *Proceedings of the National Academy of Sciences U.S.,* Vol. 41, No. 9 (1955), pp. 615–620.

we can be sure about their reliability. The cumulative circumstantial evidence, however, indicates that youngsters who are prone to become alcoholics can be spotted by the application of these and similar tests.[5]

We express the strong hope that other laboratories where interest in alcoholism exists will join in the search for the earmarks of alcoholism-proneness, and will seek to find every possible means for preventing the tendency toward alcoholism from developing into alcoholism itself.

Once potential alcoholics are spotted and are recognized as being in special danger, nutritional measures can be instituted. When people can be taught to look at the situation realistically, there will be no disgrace connected with being vulnerable as long as the vulnerable individual avoids being wounded. The only disgrace will be for those who will not heed the intelligent warning of their physicians but persist in abusing a constitution that cannot take it.

People in general, potential alcoholics and others, need to recognize the importance of being individuals. This individuality which is so important socially and politically[6] must be generally recognized so that no one will be placed in an embarrassing position because his liquor consumption does not follow a prescribed pattern set by the majority of his associates.

[5] Roger J. Williams, "Identifying and Treating Potential Alcoholics," *The Journal of Criminal Law, Criminology and Police Science,* Vol. 49, No. 3 (1958), pp. 218–221.

[6] Roger J. Williams, *Free and Unequal* (Austin, University of Texas Press, 1953).

If people's habits of thinking in these regards will yield a little, the prevention of alcoholism in young people should be much easier than the cure of confirmed cases where severe damage to the nervous tissues may make rehabilitation difficult.

How much better it will be if prevention can be accomplished!

Index

Bacteria, experiments with, 87
Barbiturates, 77, 80
Biochemical individuality, 19, 35, 43
Blood compositions: and biochemical individuality, 36; of potential
　　alcoholics, 109
Blood morphology of potential alcoholics, 109
Blood pressure and food supplements, 77
Body chemistries, distinctive, 43
Body foolishness, 18, 33, 48, 62
Body wisdom, 18, 33, 48, 62
Bone density, individuality in, 36

Calcium: hunger for, 31; body needs for, 41, 52; in vegetables, 94
Cases of alcoholism, 68
Causes of alcoholism, 16, 26, 43, 47, 63, 101, 107
Cellular metabolism, derangement of, 16
Cellular nutrition, 26, 77
Children's taste for alcohol, 13
Chromosomes and enzymes, 48
Clayton Foundation for Research, x
Coca leaves and nutrition, 80
Compartmentalization of human beings, viii
Constipation: relief by pantothenate, 50; relief by nutritional
　　supplement, 77
Control mechanisms of the body, 28
Cravings, specific physiological, 16

Deficiencies, food, effects of, 26, 33, 77
Dehydration of body tissues, 29
Dental caries, relation of, to nutrition, 52
Drug addiction, 80
Drugs, habit-forming, 17

Egg cells, nutritional requirements of, 48
Elements, ancient Greek classification of, 21
Endocrine glands: activities of, 36, 37; systems of, 54
Endocrinology, 54
Enjoyments of individuals. *See* Values in living.
Enrichment of life, diversity in, 11
Enzyme levels and biochemical individuality, 36
Enzymes in body chemistry, 36, 48
Experimental animals, use of, in alcoholism studies, 33, 47, 56

114

Food: body requirements for, 22; importance of quantitative considerations in, 23, 24. *See also* Supplements, food.

Fuel: alcohol as, 18, 19, 22, 62; body needs for, 24

Gastric juice, variations in composition of, 36

Genes and enzymes, 48

Genetotrophic concept, 46, 66

Glutamine as a food supplement, 81, 87

"Grass disease," genetotrophic origin of, 53

Habit-forming drugs, 17

Headaches and food supplements, 77

Hormones: administration of, 32, 54; production of, 55

Hypothalamus, and alcohol consumption, 18, 65, 88

Immature personality, 104

Individual cases cited, 68

Individuality: human, 19, 35, 36, 110; in rats, 58

Individuals as victims of alcoholism, 5

Insomnia, 77

Interests of individuals. *See* Values in living.

Internal tremor, 17

Intoxicating effects of alcohol, 40

Iodine, quantitative needs for, 24

Islets of Langerhans, variation in numbers, 37

Life values. *See* Values in living.

Lipoic acid as a nutrient, 83

"Lubricants" in nutrition, 62

Malformation of appetite control centers, 32

Malnutrition, 26, 33, 64, 65, 77

Meaning of alcoholism, 3, 104

Mechanisms for appetite control, 17, 29, 48, 61, 65, 88

Medical attitude, vii, 66

Mental disease and nutritional factors, 78

Mercuric chloride, skin responses to, 40

Metabolism, cellular, 16

Minerals as nutrients, 22, 82, 98

Moral responsibility of alcoholics, 92

Morphine, variation in responses to, 40, 80

Responses to drugs, variations in, 36
Rest for alcoholics, 101

Salt hunger as physiological control mechanism, 30
Satisfactions in life. *See* Values in living.
Severe cases of alcoholism, 4, 68
Smell, biochemical individuality in sense of, 40
Social adjustments, ix, 43, 101
Social pressure, 14, 102
Specific physiological cravings, 16
Statistical significance of experiments, 51
Stress and craving for alcohol, 63
Sugar: craving for, 16; deficiency causing consumption of, 33, taste for, 39
Supplements, food: treatment of alcoholics with, 67, 76, 81, 95, 96; effects of, 68, 77; attitude of alcoholics toward, 73, 75, 76; availability of, 72; cost of, 72; side effects of, 77; and blood pressure, 77; formulas for, 82, 86, 98; glutamine as, 81, 87; protein as, 93. *See also* Deficiencies, food, and Malnutrition.

Taste: of alcohol, 13, 39; responses, 38; of sugar, 39
Tensions, psychological, 14, 102, 105
Testes, variations in, 37
Thomas Nashe on alcoholics, 6
Thyroid glands, variations in, 37
Toxicities, 18, 24, 40
Treatment of alcoholics, 67, 92. *See also* Supplements, food; Alcoholics Anonymous; Religious appeal; Psychological difficulties; Psychiatry.
Triggering effect of one drink, 6, 18
"Tycopan," 67, 72, 76, 82, 86
Typical alcoholic, 7

Urine of alcoholics, 109
Utopia, game of, 8

Values in living: as revealed in game of "Utopia," 8; diversity of, 9; alcohol consumption as an example of, 10; enrichment of, 11, 93, 101
Vicious cycle, in nutrition and alcoholism, 34
Vitamin A: needs for, 41, 51; in vegetables, 94
Vitamin B_1, needs for, 42, 50